# IRMA

## A STORY OF DEVASTATION, COURAGE, AND RECOVERY

EDITORS' CHOICE

FROM THE NATION'S TOP NEWSPAPERS

TRIUMPH
BOOKS

AP Photo/David Goldman

This book is available in quantity at special discounts for your group or organization. For further information, contact:

**Triumph Books LLC**
814 North Franklin Street
Chicago, Illinois 60610
(312) 337-0747
www.triumphbooks.com

Printed in U.S.A.
ISBN: 978-1-62937-587-8
Design by Patricia Frey

With a presence in every ZIP code in America, The Salvation Army serves survivors before, during and after disasters, for however long it takes. In the aftermath of Hurricane Irma, they will continue to provide physical, emotional and spiritual support to communities as they rebuild.

A plantain field stands under water after the passing of Hurricane Maria in Yabucoa, Puerto Rico, Thursday, September 21, 2017. (AP Photo/Carlos Giusti)

# CONTENTS

Customers buy supplies and wood to secure their property in preparation of Hurricane Irma early Friday, Sept. 8, 2017 in Miami, Fla. (AP Photo/Gaston De Cardenas)

# PART 1
# BEFORE THE STORM

# SOUTH FLORIDA BRACES FOR THE WORST AS "NUCLEAR HURRICANE" NEARS

## After tearing through the Caribbean, Hurricane Irma heads toward Florida

By Evan Halper and Laura King

*Los Angeles Times* | Tribune News Service | September 7, 2017

MIAMI — Hurricane Irma took aim at South Florida on Thursday, threatening millions with historic winds, huge storm surges and unrelenting rainfall as it left behind a trail of still-uncharted devastation in the Caribbean and a death toll that climbed to at least 13.

As the monster Category 5 storm tracked west-northwest with 175-mph winds, the caprices of wind and water saved impoverished Haiti and the Dominican Republic from a direct hit. But Irma bore down late Thursday on other Caribbean targets: the low-lying Turks and Caicos, and parts of the Bahamas.

Meanwhile, the peril to the U.S. mainland grew.

"It has become more likely that Irma will make landfall in southern Florida as a dangerous major hurricane, and bring life-threatening storm surge and wind impacts to much of the state," the National Hurricane Center said.

With South Florida under a hurricane watch, Philip Levine, the mayor of vulnerable barrier-island Miami Beach, called Irma a "nuclear hurricane." Irma's leading edge was expected to reach Florida as soon as Saturday, and Gov. Rick Scott spoke of a "catastrophic storm that our state has never seen."

The hurricane has left a string of small, devastated Caribbean islands counting their dead and struggling to restore links to the outside

Residents line up at Frost Park and fill up sandbags Thursday, Sept. 7, 2017 in preparation for Hurricane Irma in Dania Beach, Fla. (Mike Stocker/South Florida Sun-Sentinel/TNS)

world. Chaotic conditions hampered efforts to compile a fatality toll, which officials said would probably grow.

The deaths included three people in the U.S. Virgin Islands and three more in Puerto Rico, their respective governors said, and the Netherlands government confirmed a fatality in St. Maarten, the shattered Dutch side of the island it shares with St. Martin, a French territory. French officials, however, revised downward from eight to four the number of people confirmed dead on the French side.

As the storm passed Puerto Rico, it dealt the U.S. territory what was in meteorological terms a glancing blow, but one that landed like a stunning punch, exacerbated by already faltering infrastructure. The governor, Ricardo Rossello, reported that a million people were left without power, and the National Weather Service in San Juan warned of flash-flooding danger from swollen rivers.

Irma's howling winds weakened slightly to 175 mph as the eye passed to the north of the Dominican Republic and Haiti. But even a sideswipe by such an intense storm carried devastating power. Hispaniola, the island the two countries share, was lashed by gales and torrential rains.

In the north of Haiti, where a hurricane last year killed some 900 people, many learned of government evacuation orders only from neighbors or relatives. Frightened people in the country's north cut branches from trees to try to shore up roofs, said Mishelle Mitchell of the humanitarian group World Vision, who was in the capital, Port-au-Prince.

In South Florida, home to some 6 million people, flight from the mighty storm that was bearing down turned chaotic at times, with the state's two main south-north arteries clogged with traffic and gasoline in short supply. Florida Highway Patrol troopers were trying to keep vehicles moving, towing disabled cars left by the roadside and escorting fuel trucks.

Florida lore is full of die-hards who ride out hurricanes, and defying a storm's fury is romanticized in films like the 1948 noir classic "Key Largo." But Scott, in a televised public briefing, pleaded with any holdouts in evacuation zones, especially in the Florida Keys, to obey orders to depart.

"Leave. Get out," the governor said, addressing those who had been told to go. "We can't save you once the storm starts."

The Keys, where a mandatory evacuation order was in place, were emptying, with 31,000 people having departed as of Thursday morning, Scott said. An advisory evacuation was in place in Miami-Dade, the state's most populous county, and the order was mandatory in low-lying areas.

The expanded evacuation zone, now encompassing about 700,000 people, covers downtown Miami and other parts of the city, plus southern parts of Miami-Dade County.

It also included Homestead, Coral Gables, South Miami, Miami Shores and North Miami Beach, authorities said.

In Miami Beach, jogger Andrea Ratkovic, 51, was preparing to head home to Oklahoma after the storm scrapped a planned trip to Barbados. First, though, she took a break from her run to help a sandbag-filling crew.

She could sympathize with what Floridians faced, she said, after living through tornadoes back home with terrifyingly high winds.

"There is little you can do to prepare for those," Ratkovic said. "You just have to run like a bug underground."

While the storm's track remained uncertain, a widening area braced for its effects. North Carolina Gov. Roy Cooper issued a statewide emergency declaration on Thursday, a day after South Carolina did so.

President Donald Trump was briefed in the Oval Office about storm preparations and Irma's projected path. Earlier, he tweeted a reminder to those in Irma's path to "be careful, be safe," as the storm approaches.

As Thursday dawned, daylight harshly illuminated the storm's destructive rampage through the hardest-hit eastern Caribbean islands, many with Colonial-era links to Western European countries.

Boats were tossed onto land. Electrical wires dangled. Streets had turned to rivers. Structures were splintered, with doors and shutters leaning at crazy angles.

Preparations on Miami Beach are underway for Hurricane Irma, as it makes its way toward Florida on Thursday, Sept. 7, 2017. (Carolyn Cole/Los Angeles Times/TNS)

"It's an enormous disaster — 95 percent of the island is destroyed," Daniel Gibbs, chairman of a local council on the French-Dutch island of St. Martin, told Radio Caribbean International.

France's interior minister, Gerard Collomb, told French radio that more dead and injured were likely to be discovered as authorities "explore all the shores."

A Dutch warship docked at St. Maarten, the Netherlands' military said. The Dutch interior minister, Ronald Plasterk, who confirmed at least one death, said there could be more casualties.

Dutch Prime Minister Mark Rutte earlier said preliminary assessments had painted a bleak picture of the storm's aftermath.

"There is no power, no gasoline, no running water," Dutch media quoted him as saying.

"Houses are underwater, cars are floating in the streets, and people are sitting in the dark, in ruined houses, cut off from the outside world."

The independent island nation of Antigua and Barbuda reported overwhelming destruction on Barbuda, with 90 percent of buildings damaged or destroyed and one death reported. Prime Minister Gaston Browne, speaking to the BBC, called it "total carnage." ∎

*Staff writer Halper reported from Miami and staff writer King from Washington. Special correspondent Les Neuhaus contributed from Homestead, Fla.*

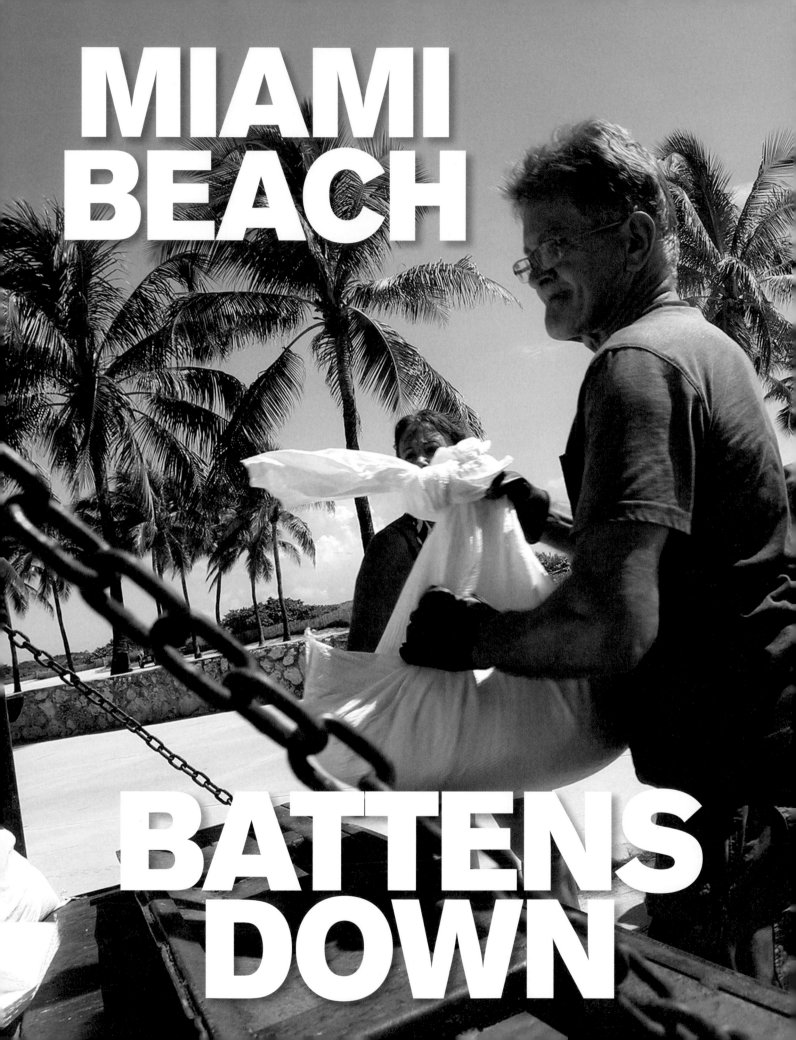

# MIAMI BEACH

# BATTENS DOWN

# Tales of sandbags, lifeguards and a monkey

### By Evan Halper

Tribune Washington Bureau | Tribune News Service | September 7, 2017

MIAMI BEACH, Fla. — Genaro Dacosta has a monkey on his back, at least sometimes. It's a small pet marmoset that may force him to ride out Hurricane Irma, now lumbering toward his home on Miami Beach.

Dacosta wants to evacuate, as the government has ordered and as most of his neighbors were doing Thursday. He's been frantically calling authorities in Tallahassee, the state capital, to get permission to bring the monkey to a shelter. So far, no luck. Hotels aren't keen on allowing monkeys, either.

So on Thursday morning, Dacosta found himself, with his family, loading sandbags into the back of his pickup. They are among a band of residents — call them stubborn, or desperate — who are going to hunker down at home, in the path of an extremely dangerous storm, and hope for the best.

"There is nothing I could do," he said. "I have what they call a 'wild animal.' I won't leave him."

Jitters aside, Miami Beach was largely calm before the storm, which is expected to hit Florida this weekend. Downtown had not yet been shuttered. Cafes were still open. Businesses were open, if slow. Tourists were getting into cabs and Ubers to leave.

Locals were quietly making preparations — either to leave or to stay.

Lifeguards used trucks to tow lifeguard stations back into the brush, in hopes they don't float away. Two sandbag stations had lines — one much longer than the other — that were calm and orderly. Volunteers and

Genaro Dacosta, age 65, of Miami Beach loads sandbags. He says he can't evacuate because he has a monkey. Preparations are underway for Hurricane Irma, as it makes its way towards Florida. (Carolyn Cole/Los Angeles Times/TNS)

city workers sweated profusely as they shoveled sand into white bags, the sun beating down.

Andrea Ratkovic, a very fit Oklahoman, had been taking one last 6-mile run before decamping with the rest of the tourist masses when she saw sandbags getting filled. She decided to stop and lend a hand.

Ratkovic has seen her share of disasters. She lives 10 miles from where one of the most intense tornadoes ever recorded touched down. Those winds were 316 mph, she said. "There is little you can do to prepare for those," she said. "You just have to run like a bug underground."

At least with a hurricane, you have some advance notice. So Ratkovic, 51, did what she could to help out. "Everybody lives somewhere where stuff happens," she said.

Her trip, with a friend, was supposed to take them to Barbados. They canceled that and diverted to Miami Beach, hoping for the best. Now they are just heading home. "I think we are getting out by the skin of our teeth," Ratkovic said.

In line for sandbags, a few cars behind Dacosta, was Charlie Garcia, who knows how much damage a hurricane can do. He was 10 when his family decided not to evacuate for Hurricane Andrew. Their house was leveled.

"It was total devastation," he said. Nevertheless, Garcia is again staying put.

"This is my home, man," he said. "Where else am I going to go? Everywhere is going to get hit."

He figured he is as safe in the high-rise where he now lives, across the street from the water, as anywhere else in South Florida. His building asked residents to collect sandbags, so that is what he was doing.

Garcia had just gotten back from the Florida Keys, where he has another home in the city of Marathon. He is expecting the worst there after seeing images of what Irma did farther south in the Caribbean.

"If it hits like that in the Keys, it will be horrible," he said. ■

People at a Red Cross shelter set up at North Miami Beach Senior High School wait in line for lunch, Friday, Sept. 8, 2017 in North Miami Beach, Fla. (AP Photo/Wilfredo Lee)

# PATIENCE IN SHORT SUPPLY AS DESPERATION SETS IN AMONG SOUTH FLORIDA RESIDENTS

## Floridians find long lines at shelters as they flee Hurricane Irma

By Evan Halper and Les Neuhaus

Tribune Washington Bureau | Tribune News Service | September 8, 2017

MIAMI — Tiffany Ceballos and her family arrived at the iron gate in front of Miami Coral Park Senior High School on Friday seeking refuge in the sturdy suburban edifice from the anticipated furies of Hurricane Irma.

But instead of being shown to a cot and a food line, they were shown the door by a National Guard soldier in camo fatigues.

The fact that Ceballos' sister had spent three hours waiting in line on behalf of the family of six, all of them fleeing Little Havana, meant nothing, they were told. Only those who were there since first thing in the morning were getting in.

"We didn't find out about the evacuation order until this morning," Ceballos protested. "We needed to pack up. We didn't expect it to fill so quick..."

As she waited for instructions on where else her family could go, Ceballos looked exasperated — and in that, she was not alone.

With hundreds of thousands of people streaming out of their homes for safety, tensions were flaring in the final, unsettling hours before Irma crashes into the city.

Life's necessities are getting increasingly harder to come by, and in some cases, they are unavailable. Displaced Miamians are losing patience with shelters that have surged over capacity, fights are breaking out at parched gas stations, and the airport was a cauldron of frayed nerves in the hours before it was to close Friday evening.

"It is impossible to get out," said Davide Corradi, who had been booked on a weekend

Tiffany Ceballos, center, from Little Havana, waits for word from members of the Florida National Guard at Miami Coral Park Senior High School, as evacuees try to get into the school, but are told there is no more room, on Friday, Sept. 8, 2017. (Carolyn Cole/Los Angeles Times/TNS)

# Many gas stations closed altogether as the city emptied out, with normally bustling streets devoid of activity. The uneasiness that settled over Miami was particularly alarming to stranded tourists.

flight back home to Milan, Italy. "I tried to change my ticket. I couldn't." With so many hotels under evacuation, he and his wife were among thousands unable to find a room.

"So we stay here," he said, pointing to a row of chairs in the airport terminal where he expected to stay until his flight finally leaves early next week.

Many stranded passengers had grueling tales of being placed on interminable hold with ticket agents, quoted exorbitant prices, and spending hours trying to purchase seats on travel websites — only to learn later that the seats did not exist.

Whether one paid $100 or $1,000 to travel just a few states away appeared to be a matter of luck. Rowan Black and his friends, all from Germany, decided to chance it and showed up at the airport at 3 a.m., hoping to find a flight anywhere out of Miami.

When the Delta ticket office finally opened up three hours later, they scored seats to Atlanta for $116. "They told us those same tickets would have been $1,000 if we bought them a day earlier," said Black, as one of his exhausted friends snoozed in a nearby terminal chair.

They probably benefited from a decision by several major airlines to cap ticket prices and temporarily suspend the algorithms they typically use that increase the prices of tickets purchased at the last minute to as high as fliers might pay. But there ultimately were just not enough tickets to go around.

Passengers stranded at the airport eventually were bused to shelters, but in many cases there wasn't enough room there either.

"I'm not sure where to go right now," said Angelica Camacho, 30, who rode her bike to the North Miami Beach High School shelter, only to be turned away. Its 1,000 beds were full by Friday afternoon. Dozens of people stood outside, confused about what shelter might take them. "I'm trying to find one still with room," she said. "It's scary."

Miami-Dade County officials announced more shelter openings on Friday, bringing the number to 45.

Meanwhile, police arranged to escort gas tankers to help ease tensions among motorists waiting angrily at filling stations. The wait exceeded an hour at many stations — if they even had gas. Horn blaring, shouting and some shoving broke out throughout the city.

"It's tough because everyone is trying to leave now," said Tanzim Adwa, 30, who was staffing the 24-hour Marathon gas station in North Miami on Friday. Waiting motorists stretched around the block, some of them periodically leaning on their horns. "Some guys were yelling at each other this morning because one thought it was his turn," Adwa said.

Many gas stations closed altogether as the city emptied out, with normally bustling streets devoid of activity. The uneasiness that settled over Miami was particularly alarming to stranded tourists. "My family in France tried to find us tickets to get out, but it was too late," said Sophie Amsellam, who was at the North Miami shelter with her daughters, ages 10 and 15. "I just want a safe place for my kids."

Police also had to show up in lots of places where they are not usually needed, to keep the order as supplies dwindled and those hoping to get what was left on the shelves sharpened their elbows.

Ten officers responded to a Home Depot near downtown, just outside the evacuation zone.

About 500 people were waiting in line to get plywood. The line was buzzing with complaints about alleged price gouging at a different hardware store down the street, which was charging $45 a sheet.

By mid-morning Home Depot's supply of plywood was gone. Customers stayed in line anyway, hopeful another truck would soon arrive.

Back at the airport, Prasoon Mohan and his wife, Rasmi Roy, both from Miami, breathed a sigh of relief when he finally secured their boarding passes. They were on the last flight out of town being offered by American Airlines.

"It's hard to get anywhere," Roy said.

Where were they willing to go? Just about anywhere they knew people. It took them days to secure a reservation, but they finally got tickets — to Milwaukee, the agent told them.

Fine. It wasn't Miami. ∎

*Neuhaus is a special correspondent.*

© 2017 Tribune Washington Bureau

Eduardo Soriano of Miami waits in a line since dawn to purchase plywood sheets at a Home Depot store in North Miami, Fla., Wednesday, Sept. 6, 2017. (AP Photo/Marta Lavandier)

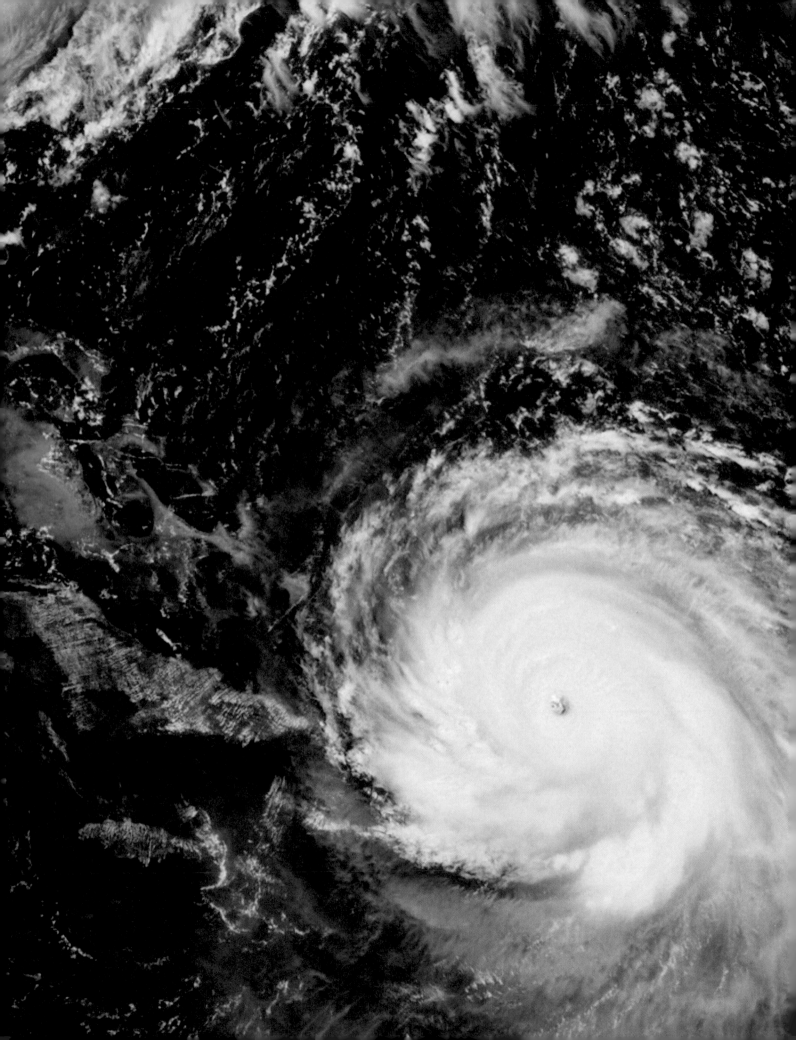

# HURRICANE IRMA: A Q&A

## How did Hurricane Irma become the second-strongest Atlantic hurricane on record?

### By Melissa Etehad and Javier Panzar

*Los Angeles Times* | Tribune News Service | September 9, 2017

Hurricane Irma, a Category 5 storm, has already made history as one of the most powerful Atlantic hurricanes on record.

Unleashing 185-mph winds and torrential rainfall, Irma has already caused death and destruction on small islands in the Caribbean and was expected to strike Florida early Sunday. States of emergency have already been declared in Puerto Rico, the U.S. Virgin Islands, Florida and South Carolina.

Here is a breakdown on hurricane strengths and how Hurricane Irma gained power.

**Question:** *What does a Category 5 storm mean?*
**A:** When meteorologists try to determine the strength of a hurricane and its potential damage to infrastructure, they rely on the Saffir-Simpson ranking. It is a scale, from 1 to 5, based on a hurricane's sustained wind speed. Here are the categories and their potential for damage, according to the National Hurricane Center:

This Monday, Sept. 4, 2017, satellite image provided by the National Oceanic and Atmospheric Administration shows Hurricane Irma nearing the eastern Caribbean. Hurricane Irma grew into a powerful Category 4 storm Monday. (NOAA via AP)

Category 1: Winds range from 74 mph to 95 mph, with the potential to uproot trees and damage roofs and power lines.

Category 2: Winds become "extremely dangerous," reaching up to 110 mph. Damage to property is also much more likely and power outages are expected.

Category 3: Considered major storms, Category 3 hurricanes are likely to produce "devastating damage." Wind speed could go up to 129 mph, resulting in damaged buildings and power outages that could last for days.

Category 4: Wind speeds can go up to 156 mph. "Catastrophic damage" is expected in areas hit hardest. Hurricane Harvey was a category 4 storm when it struck Texas.

Category 5: Storms with winds of 157 mph or higher are ranked in this category. Hurricane Andrew, one of the most destructive hurricanes recorded, was a Category 5 storm that struck Florida in 1992, killing 25 people and destroying 28,000 homes.

### Q: What makes Hurricane Irma so powerful?

A: Hurricane season officially lasts from June 1 to Nov. 30, but the peak of the season, from mid-August to early September, is when strong hurricanes such as Irma typically occur.

There are certain ingredients needed to create a powerful hurricane.

Part of that perfect recipe includes warm ocean water and little wind shear — which refers to changing wind direction. For instance, the more strong winds change direction, the more they prevent a hurricane from organizing. Less change in wind direction allows the storm to brew and gain strength, according to John Brost, meteorologist with the National Weather Service.

A hurricane also gains strength when it passes over warm water in deep parts of the ocean, and waters have been warm this season.

Another reason for Hurricane Irma's strength: Nothing has stood in its way to disrupt it, such as dry air, according to Brian Haus, a professor at the University of Miami's Rosentstiel School of Marine and Atmospheric Science.

"When dry air comes into the storm, it impedes transfer of heat," Haus said. Heat can allow a hurricane "to grow quickly and become powerful."

The speed in which a hurricane travels also affects its intensity. Hurricane Irma is moving at around 16 mph, slowly enough to utilize the energy it gets from the warm water and intensify before it hits land, Brost said.

### Q: How does Hurricane Irma compare to other storms?

A: With all those ingredients in place, Hurricane Irma's winds have peaked at 185 mph, making it the second-strongest Atlantic hurricane on record. Hurricane Allen in 1980 was the strongest Atlantic hurricane, with winds reaching 190 mph.

Another indicator about how strong a hurricane can become is the pressure at the eye of the storm. The lower the pressure, the stronger the hurricane.

Hurricane Irma ranks at the 12th-lowest pressure of all time for hurricanes in the Atlantic Ocean, and Hurricane Allen ranked as fifth, said Brost. Hurricane Wilma in 2005 came in at No. 1 in terms of lowest pressure. Wilma, a Category 3, led to around $20 billion in damage.

### Q: What role does climate change play in these storms?

A: It is hard to pin down the relationship between global climate change and any given storm.

Storms are short-lived and relatively rare, meaning there isn't a whole lot of data from which to detect trends and draw conclusions. A federal

# Scientists agree that rising sea temperatures will likely increase the number of "very intense" storms in the future.

GOES-EAST RAINBOW IR CH. 4 - SEP 5 17 01:15 UTC

In this geocolor GOES-16 satellite image taken Thursday, Sep. 7, 2017, at 11:15 a.m. EDT, shows the eye of Hurricane Irma just north of the island of Hispaniola. (NOAA-NASA via AP)

report released this year as part of the National Climate Assessment said that when it came to looking back at past storm data, "the trend signal has not yet had time to rise above the background variability of natural processes."

But scientists agree that rising sea temperatures will likely increase the number of "very intense" storms in the future.

The federal report said that computer modeling indicates an increase in tropical cyclone intensity in a warmer world.

That is because when the ocean's surface temperature rises, the atmosphere's ability to hold moisture goes up. So a hurricane moving over a warmer ocean will be able to bring in more moisture over land — increasing the chances of heavier rainfall and flooding.

Michael Mann, a climate scientist at Pennsylvania State University, wrote about this in an op-ed after Hurricane Harvey hit Houston.

"Harvey was almost certainly more intense than it would have been in the absence of human-caused warming, which means stronger winds, more wind damage and a larger storm surge," he wrote. ■

© 2017 Los Angeles Times

# WHEN HURRICANE IRMA VEERED TOWARD NAPLES, IT WAS TOO LATE TO EVACUATE

## Storm's late movement caught some residents off guard

### By Evan Halper

Tribune Washington Bureau | Tribune News Service | September 9, 2017

NAPLES, Fla. — Underneath the historic pier near downtown Naples on Saturday, Katie Alvarez hugged her son Jordan and sobbed.

Hurricanes are part of an Alvarez family tradition. Katie Alvarez has photos of her children on the pier before and after every major storm that has affected the coastal southwest Florida city. Sometimes they take photos during the storm. She was there Saturday to snap the before shots of her now-grown children.

Alvarez was in tears because she was certain there will be no photographs after the storm this year.

"It's going to be gone," said the Naples native, who joined her family at the beach in a homemade "Irma You Suck" shirt and visor with the Confederate flag emblazoned on it. She knows hurricanes from her work at a company that installs storm shutters.

"I wanted to see it one last time," Alvarez said of the pier, first built in 1888 but destroyed more than once by hurricanes over the years.

Florida has been bracing for Hurricane Irma for days, but the westward shift of the storm caught this manicured Gulfside town, known for its yachts, quaint canals and beachfront mansions, off guard. By Saturday, it was directly in Irma's path. Naples wasn't ready for this.

Not long after the nearby city of Estero opened a 7,500-bed shelter at the Germain Arena, its immense parking lot was teeming with evacuees. The line snaked up and down, and it appeared there might be more people than beds. Other shelters were filling up quickly, leaving city officials scrambling to prepare new locations.

"They didn't tell us we were being evacuated until the very last minute," said Barbara Sobol, a 70-year-old Cape Coral resident who looked deflated as she took a timeout from the hours-

Barbara Sabol, 70, of Cape Coral, Fla., waits to get into a shelter in Estero on Saturday, Sept. 9, 2017. She said she left her cat at home because she was worried about all the dogs at the shelter. (Carolyn Cole/Los Angeles Times/TNS)

long wait in line, while her husband kept their place. Just minutes earlier, an elderly woman had fainted and was taken away by an ambulance, suffering from what seemed a bout of heat exhaustion.

The line was filled with yapping pooches, which were permitted to accompany their owners inside. But Sobol said the commotion of the shelter would have probably upset her cat more than the commotion of riding out Irma in an empty house. "I left food for her at high elevations in different places. She'll find it," Sobol said. "This shelter is a strange, noisy place. She'd be scared here."

In the hours before the storm's expected arrival in South Florida, million-dollar boats floated helplessly at the Naples Boat Club. Susan Boucek, the owner of a gorgeous vintage sailboat, said she would be staying put in one of the club's apartments feet away from the water — a risky move. But Boucek refuses to abandon ship. She and other boat owners were frantically securing their vessels to 12-foot-high pillars in the water, placing the knots at the very top in anticipation of the floating dock rising that high as storm-surge waters flood in.

"We were all posed with the same problem," said Bill Charbonneau, as he tied down the 86- and 75-foot Sunseeker yachts he charters for cruises. "It was hard to escape in any direction." The twists and turns of the storm were too hard to predict. He is hoping the yachts will live up to their names: Perseverance I and II.

Charbonneau's phone has been ringing off the hook as the storm bears down. Potential clients want to lock him in to take them to see their battered mansions in the Florida Keys after the storm passes — if Charbonneau's yachts make it themselves.

"Obviously, that is not where you want to get your business," he said.

The area was abuzz with talk of boat owners in Miami and nearby cities who had schlepped their vessels to the Gulf Coast thinking they would escape Irma's worst. Instead, their boats appeared to be suddenly in the storm's direct path.

For many locals in and around Naples who wanted to get out, there simply wasn't time. By

Saturday morning, one forecaster was warning that the next day would bring tornado-force winds. Even the weather forecaster said he's leaving his condominium because he feared the roof would blow off.

Elderly residents who previously managed to escape other storms found themselves unable to leave town; it was too late. There is only one interstate leading out of harm's way from this corner of the state, and it was jammed with other evacuees. Local officials advised residents to seek refuge instead at local shelters, which were quickly filling up. Those who heard from friends who had managed to pack up their cars and hit the highway repeated stories of 13-hour drives just to get to the state line.

"This is the first time we have come to a shelter," said Ann Johnson, 82, as she sat with her husband and another couple under the fluorescent lights of the Palmetto Ridge High School cafeteria. "Usually we just pack up and go. We looked at the timing of this and realized there was nowhere to go. This is as safe a place as any."

Although not very comfortable. Johnson slept across three stiff plastic chairs the night before. There weren't enough cots for everyone. Only the infirm were given a bed.

Pat and Dennis Boyle, another elderly couple, had been tracking the storm closely and thought they would be safe in their inland home. They, too, ended up at the shelter.

"We couldn't get anywhere else," said Dennis Boyle, 87. "The problem with trying to leave is you can get on the interstate and run out of gas. All the gas stations are closed. What do you do then?"

By the pier, locals anxiously plotted their plans for making it through the torrent. "My house is awful old," said Peter Hinrichs, 80, as he chatted with a neighbor and a city maintenance worker.

"I'm afraid it is going to blow away. Everything I own is in it," said Hinrichs, who was heading to his daughter's more-secure home to ride out Irma's wrath.

Hinrichs did not even consider leaving town. "I'm 80 years old," he said. "I start to fall asleep on long drives. It's more dangerous on the road than it is for me here."

Thousands of people wait to get into Germain Arena in Estero, Fla., as the mandatory evacuation orders, prompted by Hurricane Irma, are extended in the area of Naples and Ft. Myers on Saturday, Sept. 9, 2017. (Carolyn Cole/Los Angeles Times/TNS)

His friend Gary Sharp, who also is staying, chimed in: "They say the roads are an even bigger mess than this thing is going to be," he said.

They were standing in a parking lot that was sure to be under water by Sunday. In fact, it was just drying out from flooding related to residual surges caused by Hurricane Harvey, which hit Texas two weeks ago. What would be left of the rest of the town was a big question mark.

"We don't know," Sharp said. "Nobody knows."

"Weather is unpredictable, like everything else in life," said Courtney Vernon, 31, who stayed to look after her family's beach home, smack in the path of a surge zone where water levels are anticipated to rise 10 feet. She planned to decamp for a shelter once the storm arrived. Vernon was holding out hope for another shift in the storm that would move it away from the area. That was looking unlikely.

Whether Sherri Bourdo and Anthony Guidry would flee his beachfront home remained a matter of debate between the couple. He wanted to stick it out, against the advice of every government official and repeated warnings that rescue crews would not be able to reach them there. She was thinking that may not be too smart.

"We might have to make a last-minute decision to stay at a friend's house," Guidry allowed.

Bourdo moved to Naples from the Midwest earlier in the year. On Saturday morning, she was still trying to process what was about to hit.

"It's been kind of surreal," she said. "This is all new to me." Bourdo stood on the pier, catching one last glimpse of the vista before the storm. "Gas lines and lines to buy water are not something I have seen before."

Nor has she seen an ocean pier there one day, and likely gone the next. ∎

© 2017 Tribune Washington Bureau

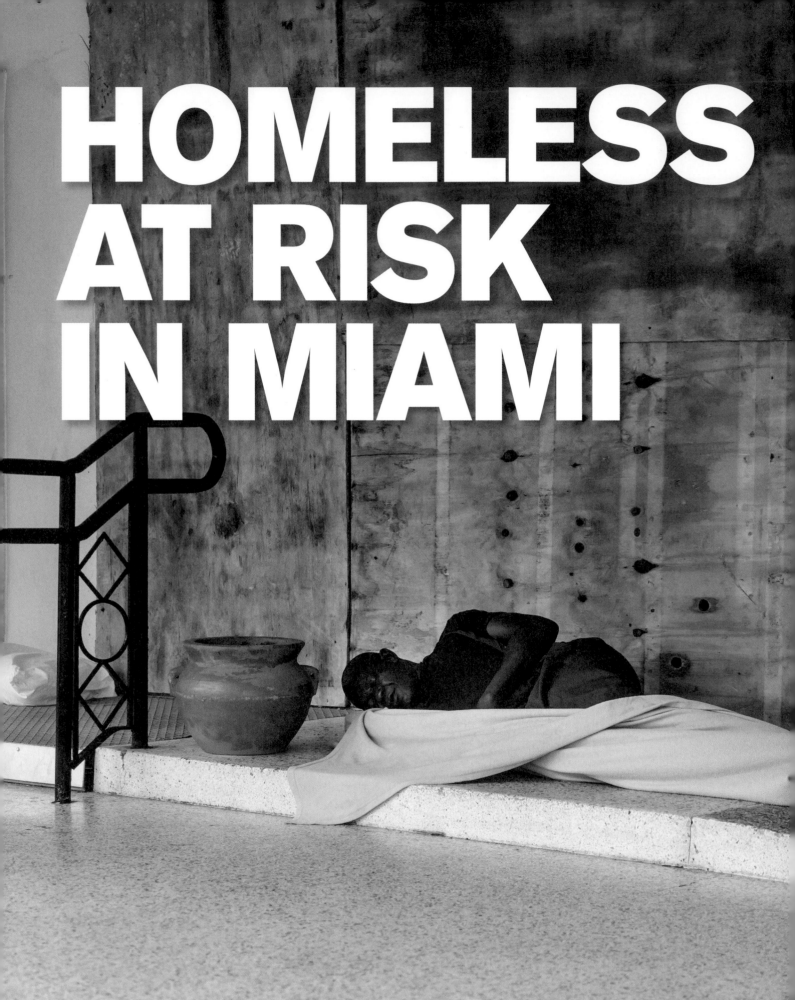

# HOMELESS AT RISK IN MIAMI

# Area's homeless population among most vulnerable to Hurricane Irma

### By Les Neuhaus and Kurtis Lee
*Los Angeles Times* | Tribune News Service
September 9, 2017

MIAMI — While Miami was mostly evacuated by Saturday, one group still had a noticeable presence: the homeless.

"I'll be all right," Terry Donald, who estimated he had been living on the streets here for two years, said as he shuffled barefoot down a deserted downtown street. "I think I'll make it through."

In the hours before Hurricane Irma was expected to pummel Florida, authorities were urging homeless people to go to shelters.

For those who refused, police were employing a controversial law known as the Baker Act, which allows officers to send anybody they believe poses a danger to themselves or others to a mental institution, where they can be held for up to 72 hours for an involuntary examination.

The 1971 law has been widely criticized by advocates for the homeless. But with Irma bearing down on Miami-Dade County, some advocates had been urging local authorities to use it.

"It's a bad storm and we needed to take drastic measures," said Ron Book, chairman of the Miami-

A homeless man sleeps outside a boarded storefront in Miami Beach on Saturday, Sept. 9, 2017, as Hurricane Irma approaches. (Marcus Yam/Los Angeles Times/TNS)

Dade County Homeless Trust, a public-private partnership that aims to end homelessness. "I'm not going to see our homeless population dead in the streets.

"I'd rather see this law used than to have them in body bags," he said.

Book's group estimates about 1,130 people are homeless in Miami-Dade County. He said that on Friday law enforcement officials invoked the Baker Act to take six people off the streets.

"For almost two weeks we've been telling people living on the streets this storm is headed here and it's going to be bad," he said.

On Saturday afternoon, scores of homeless people were walking the streets, tucked under building awnings and sleeping on sidewalks.

A *Los Angeles Times* reporter witnessed several homeless people being loaded into a police van.

Jerry Dean, who said he'd been homeless for four months in Miami, said he was happy to get the help.

"There's no way to ride this storm out — it ain't going to happen," said Dean, 50, of New Jersey. "This storm will kill you."

Deborah Ford, who sat in her wheelchair, paralyzed from the waist down, said there wasn't much choice for her.

"What am I going to do?" said Ford, 62. The police "are just doing their job for the most part. A lot of people don't want to come off the streets."

James Bernat Sr., a senior executive assistant to the Miami police chief and the department's point person on homeless issues, said that some homeless people were being taken to shelters. Any removed from the streets under the Baker Act would be taken to Jackson Memorial Hospital for evaluation, he said.

"This is to ensure their safety and the safety of the public," he said.

The use of the law to evacuate people was not universally praised by homeless advocates.

The National Coalition for the Homeless said in a statement that it rejects the "misconception that all homeless folks have a mental illness or that someone who has a mental illness does not understand the danger of a storm like Irma."

"People who are homeless are survivors," the statement said. "We are concerned that Miami's decision to invoke the Baker Act sends the wrong message about how we respect the rights of those who do not have a home." ∎

*Neuhaus, a special correspondent, reported from Miami, and* Times *staff writer Lee reported from Los Angeles.*

An official in Miami speaks with homeless people about moving to shelters ahead of powerful Hurricane Irma on Sept. 8, 2017. (AP Photo/Josh Replogle)

John Duke wades through a flooded street to try to salvage his flooded car in the wake of Hurricane Irma, Monday, Sept. 11, 2017, in Jacksonville, Fla. (AP Photo/John Bazemore)

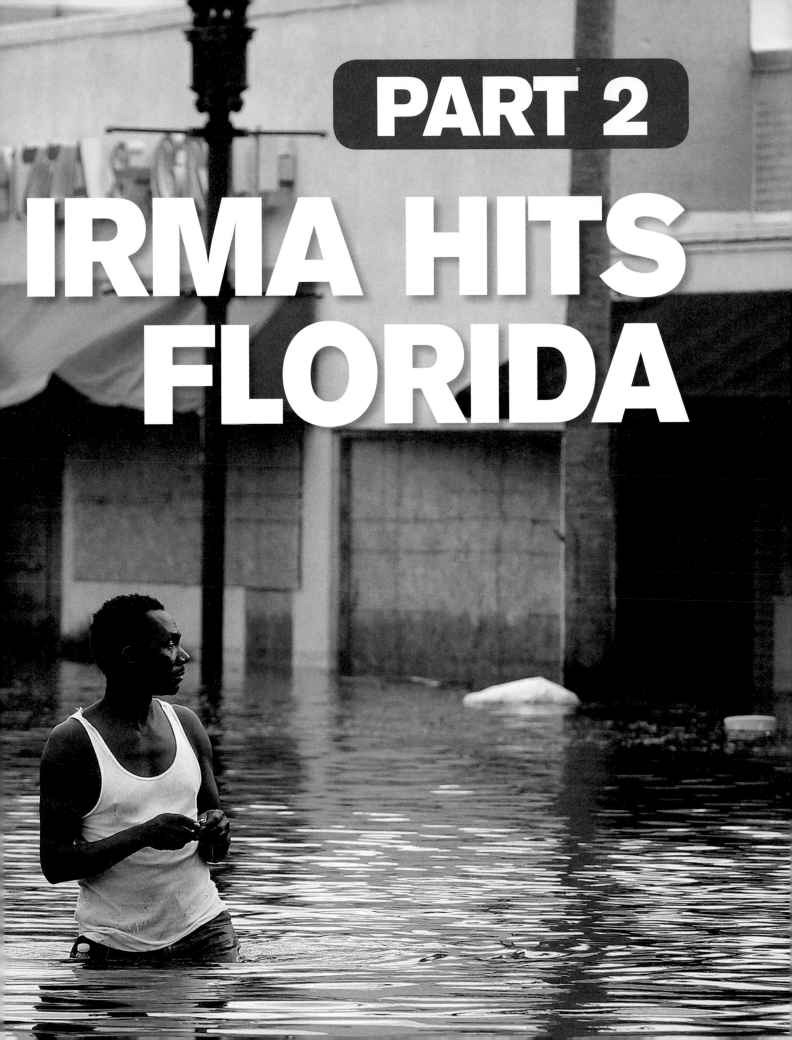

# PART 2

# IRMA HITS FLORIDA

# FIRST HURRICANE-FORCE WINDS
# HIT FLORIDA KEYS

## Irma bears down on the Florida Keys

### By John Cherwa and Evan Halper

*Los Angeles Times* | Tribune News Service | September 10, 2017

NAPLES, Fla. — The Florida Keys began to feel the wrath of Hurricane Irma on Saturday night as the powerful storm headed on a collision course with the western coast of Florida, which braced for a potentially devastating day of deadly winds and surging seas.

Irma was expected to unleash its full fury of 125 mph winds sometime around sunrise over Key West, barring a sudden change in direction, with the Fort Myers-Naples area in the storm's relentless cross hairs by mid-afternoon.

Hurricane-force gusts were already blasting the spindly islands of the Keys Saturday night, while escalating winds, driving rain and isolated tornadoes surged across Florida on the massive storm's leading edge.

Miami, which on Friday was launching a massive evacuation in anticipation of a direct hit, was breathing easier as the storm tracked west yet Irma's 350-mile-wide girth meant the city was still in for 90 mph winds and a storm surge of 3 to 6 feet.

Nearly 7 million people were under advice to evacuate many of those on the west coast unable to because with the storm's change of direction the warning came too late.

State transportation officials allowed cars to use the shoulders traveling the bumper-to-bumper highway out of Tampa; in Naples and Fort Myers, where many buildings weren't constructed to withstand the expected storm surge, people fled to crowded shelters by the thousands.

An American flag is torn as Hurricane Irma passes through Naples, Fla., Sunday, Sept. 10, 2017. (AP Photo/David Goldman)

"The storm is here," Gov. Rick Scott said. "Hurricane Irma is now impacting our state. ... This is a deadly storm and the state has never seen anything like it."

The massive movement of water onto ordinarily dry land that is expected could have life-threatening consequences, state and federal officials warned.

"There is a serious threat of significant storm surge flooding along the entire west coast of Florida and this has increased to 15 feet above ground level," Scott said. "Fifteen feet is devastating and will cover your house."

The National Weather Service warned that the storm was so large in size hurricane-force winds could be expected throughout south and central Florida no matter which side of the state one was on.

"This is as real as it gets," the service said in a statement.

Still, a change in wind direction prevented the storm from intensifying on its approach to Florida as originally had been anticipated, and instead of making landfall as a Category 4 storm, it was anticipated to remain at a Category 3 level, with comparatively slower winds.

Landfall on Florida's west coast, possibly near Fort Myers, would bring winds of about 120 mph, the National Weather Service said late Saturday night.

Still, people along Florida's western coast spent the day scrambling for shelter.

Near Naples, locals waited in an hours-long line to get inside the Germain Arena in Estero, which had become a 7,500-bed shelter. Many of them had avoided such shelters in previous storms and would not have been there Saturday if their neighborhoods hadn't abruptly been evacuated.

The evacuation zone grew so large by Saturday morning that even those who had made arrangements to stay in hotels were sent to shelters because the hotels were being evacuated.

Staying at home was out of the question for Elizabeth and John Simler, whose house is built on land about 5 feet above sea level on Sanibel Island,

The surf floods a walkway leading to the beach as Hurricane Irma passes through Naples, Fla., Sunday, Sept. 10, 2017. (AP Photo/David Goldman)

with the stilts it sits on boosting the home an additional 10 feet.

They had prepared, they thought.

"We had a very fine hotel reservation," said Elizabeth, 57. "We did not expect to be in this line (at the shelter)."

The hotel alerted them only hours before that guests were being turned away.

Lou Fusco bailed on his hotel before it could bail on him.

"They said if there is a forced evacuation, you will have to leave," he said. "So I said, 'If that happens, then where the hell am I going to go?'"

Even in Miami, residents were worried about what possible 90 mph winds would do to the city.

In downtown Miami Beach, Jose Toledo, a 27-year-old sound design engineer, said he was moving out of his ninth-floor apartment along the waterfront because it didn't have shutters.

"We're going to stay in my office because it's safer there," he said while emerging for a few last-minute supplies. "The construction down here isn't good. I'm worried about things flying off the buildings ... and you've got all these construction sites with loose stuff on the ground. It could be dangerous for sure."

About 75,000 people were registered at shelters by Saturday night.

As the first heavy winds blew in, there were reports of electrical transformers exploding and downed trees.

As of Saturday night, almost 200,000 homes had lost power, and officials have predicted that total outages could reach 4 million before Irma heads into Georgia on Monday.

Hurricane warnings were issued all the way up the east and west coasts of Florida, with hurricane watches pending in Georgia and lower South Carolina. Tropical storm watches were declared along the Florida Panhandle and mid-coastal South Carolina.

Seven counties in south Florida were under a tornado watch; a full-out warning was issued in the Miami-Dade County area after two tornados were spotted there. More counties were expected to be added as the initial bands from the storm reached those areas.

Several cities, including Miami, were imposing nighttime curfews as the storm approached. Most central Florida counties planned to do the same on Sunday night.

Every major airport in Florida was closed with the exception of Tallahassee and Pensacola. Tallahassee planned to shut down on Monday.

Saturday's urgency was foreshadowed by the damage done to Cuba on Friday and Saturday and other Caribbean islands earlier in the week. The death toll was at least 25.

Cuba's meteorological agency reported that Irma came ashore Friday night in central Camaguey province, home to the country's third-largest city, with winds so strong that they destroyed measurement instruments.

Hurricane-strength winds were later recorded in the northern half of Camaguey. Irma was the first Category 5 hurricane to hit the province in 85 years, according to state media. Damage was reported across the province, the station said: roofs torn off, trees downed and power disconnected.

In the province of Holguin, some families took shelter in caves to ride out the storm.

"No one wants to leave the house, only silence is interrupted by gusts of wind and rain," Yoani Sanchez, who runs a Havana-based digital news service, 14ymedio, tweeted about the situation in Camaguey.

Sanchez posted photos of people crowding the streets of Havana to pray. She reported that supplies were running low.

Irma was eventually downgraded to Category 3 before it headed for Florida on Saturday.

The storm is one of three hurricanes cycling through the warm September waters. Hurricane Katia struck the eastern coast of Mexico early Saturday as a Category 1 storm. Luis Felipe Puente, head of Mexico's national emergency services agency, said two people were killed by the hurricane, which roared onshore in Veracruz state, pelting the region with intense rains and winds. ∎

© 2017 Los Angeles Times

From left, firefighters Dohnovan Simpson and Jacob McGovern carry Dolores Gevaza, 83, across the courtyard in the rain at John Hopkins Middle School on Sunday, Sept. 10, 2017, in St. Petersburg, Fla. (Eve Edelheit/Tampa Bay Times via AP)

# HURRICANE IRMA CONTINUES ITS ASSAULT ON SOUTHEAST FLORIDA

## Rain, wind and storm surges endanger residents

By David Fleshler

*Sun Sentinel* | Tribune News Service | September 10, 2017

FORT LAUDERDALE, Fla. — Hurricane Irma retained its 130 mph strength early Sunday afternoon as its eye crossed the Florida Keys and headed toward the Gulf coast, where Naples, Fort Myers and Tampa rushed preparations for the Category 4 storm's arrival.

The storm, already huge, grew wider overnight, with hurricane-force winds extending across 160 miles and tropical-force winds extending across 440 miles.

Although the forecast for South Florida improved, the region still faced a day of hazardous weather, with the worst of it coming Sunday through late afternoon.

Strong gusts uprooted trees and knocked down branches. Gusts near 90 mph were reported off Key Biscayne. More than 1.25 million South Florida customers lost power. A construction crane was blown over in downtown Miami. A 69 mph gust was recorded at Palm Beach International Airport early Sunday afternoon.

Although a storm surge warning for Broward and Palm Beach counties was been canceled, heavy rain was expected, with 6 to 8 inches possible in coastal Palm Beach County and 8 to 10 inches in Broward and central Palm Beach.

"This is a serious, still life-threatening event," Broward County Mayor Barbara Sharief said. "Our community has coastal areas and low-lying areas that are going to be subject to widespread flooding, on top of extensive wind damage."

The storm landed on Cudjoe Key, about 20 miles from Key West, at 9:10 a.m. Sunday, the National Hurricane Center said. A gust of 120 mph was recorded at nearby Big Pine Key, home of the National Key Deer Refuge.

"It's wicked, this is unbelievable," said Vic Lamorte, bunkered in a hurricane-shuttered three-story concrete house in Tavernier in the Middle Keys, in a telephone interview. "When I say whipping, I mean it's whipping outside. And it's howling, unbelievable howling."

A man stands in a flooded street on the waterfront of Fort Lauderdale, Fla., to take photos as Hurricane Irma passes through on Sunday, September 10, 2017. (Paul Chiasson/The Canadian Press via AP)

In South Florida Saturday night, streets glistened with rain and became free of vehicles as curfews were imposed at 4 p.m. Saturday in Broward, 3 p.m. in Palm Beach and 7 p.m. in the city of Miami.

A "large and dangerous tornado" swept west through central Broward County toward the Everglades Saturday evening, the National Weather Service said. Other tornado reports came in, as powerful rotating thunderstorms from the hurricane's outer bands led the weather service to issue tornado warnings across Broward, Miami-Dade and Palm Beach counties.

Shelters filled up across South Florida, as mandatory evacuations emptied coastal neighborhoods. In Palm Beach County, more than 16,000 people planned to sleep at the county's 15 shelters — about a third of the county's capacity. Broward opened extra shelters.

As the storm moved north Sunday, it was forecast to flood coastal neighborhoods of southwest Florida with a storm surge of 10 to 15 feet.

"Irma is expected bring life-threatening wind and storm surge to the Florida Keys and southwestern Florida as an extremely dangerous major hurricane tonight through Sunday," the hurricane center said.

Hurricane Irma could dump as much as 20 inches of rain on parts of Palm Beach County, said Bill Johnson, director of emergency management.

"That is a significant amount of rain for Palm Beach County," said Bill Johnson, Palm Beach County's director of emergency management. "But it won't be anything like Houston." ∎

© 2017 Sun Sentinel

A man walks through accumulated algae on the waterfront of Fort Lauderdale, Fla., as Hurricane Irma passes through on Sunday, September 10, 2017. (Paul Chiasson/The Canadian Press via AP)

# HURRICANE IRMA'S CALAMITOUS SWEEP THROUGH FLORIDA – AND IT'S NOT OVER YET

## Unpredictable storm blows across Florida coast

By Patrick J. McDonnell, Laura King and Evan Halper

*Los Angeles Times* | Tribune News Service | September 10, 2017

NAPLES, Fla. — In a calamitous northward sweep from the Everglades to the Florida Panhandle, a weakening but still monstrously powerful Hurricane Irma battered a string of cities on the state's palm-fringed west coast Sunday before advancing toward Georgia and the Carolinas.

Irma, downgraded Sunday afternoon to a Category 2 storm and expected to lose its hurricane status Monday, yielded watery misery and hours of scouring winds even in areas that avoided a direct hit, like Miami, and flattened buildings in the Florida Keys, where it first made landfall.

So broad and punishing was the storm's reach that no corner of Florida, the country's fourth most-populous state, was unaffected.

And Irma was an avatar of night terrors: As darkness fell, the storm was bearing down on the populous Tampa Bay region, rendered especially vulnerable to deadly storm surges by the bay's funnel shape.

There were at least four deaths. A man in the Florida Keys drove his car into a light pole, and a woman driving on a toll road in central Florida ran into a rail. In a rural area southeast of Tampa, two law enforcement officers died after their vehicles crashed head-on. None of the incidents was linked conclusively to the storm.

As the storm moved over land, losing punch but gaining speed, a slight tack to the northeast imperiled the theme park destination of Orlando, and the center of the state saw repeated Irma-spawned tornadoes.

A car sits on flooded Collier Avenue, Monday, Sept. 11, 2017, in downtown Everglades City, Fla. (Douglas R. Clifford/Tampa Bay Times via AP)

With more than 3 million homes and businesses without power and a vast reckoning of the destruction still at hand, President Donald Trump moved to free up funds for a huge rebuilding effort.

"Right now we're worried about lives, not cost," he told reporters as he returned to the White House from a weekend at the presidential retreat of Camp David.

Sunday's dizzying sequence of stormy weather saw dual landfalls by the hurricane over a span of little more than six hours. After striking the Keys in midmorning, the eye of the storm moved over Marco Island, south of Naples. And soon after came the floodwaters, with water levels in Naples increasing 7 feet in just 90 minutes.

As the storm's trajectory took it north, water was sucked from part of Tampa Bay, exposing a muddy expanse that would normally be underwater — a frightening portent of flooding to come when that water, and more, comes rushing back.

"MOVE AWAY FROM THE WATER!" appealed the National Hurricane Center after photos on social media showed people and dogs frolicking on the bay's exposed sand.

The cities bracketing Tampa Bay — Tampa and St. Petersburg, with a population of some 3 million people between them — were forecast to be clobbered later Sunday by sustained hurricane-force winds. A direct hit on the area would be the first in nearly a century.

"We are about to get punched in the face by this storm," declared Tampa Mayor Bob Buckhorn.

The storm's passage by no means marks the end of the danger. "Once this system passes through, it's going to be a race to save lives and sustain lives," William B. "Brock" Long, the Federal Emergency Management Agency administrator, said on "Fox News Sunday."

Samantha Belk says goodbye to her maltese, Gardolf, until after the hurricane in a locker room at John Hopkins Middle School on Sunday, Sept. 10, 2017, in St. Petersburg, Fla. The school filled classrooms and hallways with people evacuating Hurricane Irma. (Eve Edelheit/Tampa Bay Times via AP)

**45**

With the storm on a havoc-filled trajectory, much of Florida was a jumbled tableau of overflowing shelters, boarded-up buildings and deserted streets in normally bustling urban centers. Palm trees blew sideways, with fronds snapping under the assault; tree branches flew like missiles.

In Pinellas County, which encompasses St. Petersburg, officials announced a curfew, and sheriff's deputies hurried to relocate 1,000 inmates from the Pinellas County Jail.

An overnight curfew was also announced in Miami, where almost horizontal sheets of rain whipped through downtown all day long, and the wind seemed to come simultaneously from all directions. Whitecaps were visible on Brickell Avenue, a main north-south waterfront artery, and other major streets flooded as well.

The wind made weapons of debris and even coconuts from palm trees, and powerful gusts threatened some two dozen construction cranes dotting Miami. At least two collapsed in Sunday's winds.

By nighttime in Miami, the winds, while still fierce, had diminished to the point where it was possible to stand outside without tumbling over, and the rain had given way to clearing skies. A few people ventured outside, some walking their cooped-up dogs.

For those sheltering in hotels, board games and boredom — a contrast to the angry panorama outside — carried the day. "It's fine; at least it's safer than the house," said Chris McShane, who was staying at a Homewood Suites in the Brickell area in downtown Miami with his wife, Jennifer, and their children, Ashley, 1 and Riley, 2, after the family fled their home in the city's north.

Amid the storm's ravages came small points of light. A woman in Miami's Little Haiti neighborhood went into labor and emergency responders were unable to reach her, so doctors coached her through the birth by phone, the city of Miami reported on Twitter. Sunday morning, mother and baby — a girl — were safely transported to Jackson Hospital by fire crews, the city reported.

In Florida alone, more than 6.5 million people were told to flee in advance of the storm, leading to days of jam-packed highways and frantic searches for gasoline amid one of the nation's largest emergency evacuations ever. More than half a million others were ordered to evacuate in Georgia.

In downtown Fort Myers, on Florida's southwest coast, the hurricane's leading edge was so strong that it was hard to walk a block. Ominously, the Caloosahatchee River's level dropped sharply, its lowered tide likely heralding a storm surge.

Some seemed ill-equipped to face an epic weather event, armed with little more than bravado.

"I got rum, cheese, tortillas," announced Michael Gandy, a sunburned 77-year-old, who was keeping an eye on his boat from a marina-side apartment complex in Fort Myers.

People who had left everything they owned behind could only worry and wait as the wind and water reached a crescendo. "I'm worried I won't have a house to go back to," said Diana Frana, who fled her canal-side home in Cape Coral, on Fort Myers' outskirts.

Florida's lifeblood is tourism, so the storm-stranded included many from out of state — and from outside the U.S. An Argentine family, the Mureoccas, spent a week at Walt Disney World, but were thwarted when they tried to fly back to Buenos Aires after visiting Miami Beach.

"It's not what we planned," said Leonardo Mureocca, 44, who was stuck at a hotel near Miami's airport with his wife and two daughters, 8 and 12. "This is our first hurricane — we don't have this kind of thing."

By the time the storm hit, Floridians had already had a grim preview of Irma's fury: The storm left a trail of destruction across the eastern Caribbean, barreling up through the lush Leeward Islands and killing at least two dozen people.

More than 36 hours after being pummeled by what was still then a Category 5 storm, a shaken Cuba was still assessing the damage Sunday. Initially, the storm had not been expected to make landfall there, but it passed directly over northern islands, with effects felt as far away as the capital, Havana. Passing over Cuba probably weakened the storm as it punched onward toward Florida, scientists said.

Even while the storm raged, there were sober assessments of a long and painful recovery for the storm zone on the U.S. mainland. Sen. Bill Nelson, D-Fla., speaking on CNN, said weeks and months of disruption are to be expected.

"This storm has covered the whole state of Florida," he said, predicting a "slow slog" back to any semblance of normalcy.

A determined few Floridians seized any opportunity — even a fleeting one like the hurricane's eye, a period of relative calm — to check on homes and property.

John Krowzow, who is 74, slipped away to check on the situation in Corkscrew Woodlands, a mobile home park for seniors in Estero, a hard-hit town near Fort Myers.

"I feel good!" he said after finding that his mobile home, raised on cinder blocks, was intact. ∎

© 2017 Los Angeles Times

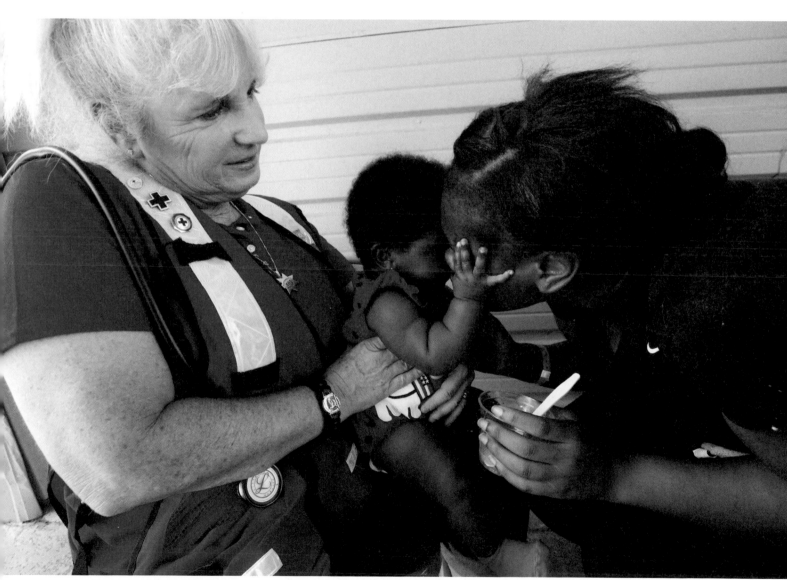

Janay Washington, right, 20, of North Miami Beach, Fla., gives her five-month-old daughter Ke'Lanni a hug as Red Cross nurse Liz Miller, of Placerville, Calif., helps feed her at a Red Cross hurricane shelter set up in the Miami-Dade County Fair Expo Center, Tuesday, Sept. 19, 2017, in Miami. The Washingtons were rescued as rising floodwaters surrounded their home during Hurricane Irma. Only about 450 evacuees remain in the shelter as many are going back to their homes or transitioning back to shelters in the Florida Keys. (AP Photo/Wilfredo Lee)

# CUBA MAY HAVE SPARED FLORIDA FROM WORSE DAMAGE

## Island nation takes brunt of Hurricane Irma

### By Kate Linthicum

*Los Angeles Times* | Tribune News Service | September 11, 2017

MEXICO CITY — Nieves Martinez Burgaleta, 87, was found floating in the flooded streets outside her home in Havana.

Alberto Flores Garcia, 77, was crushed to death by a utility pole uprooted by hurricane winds.

Yolendis Castillo Martinez, 27, died when a balcony damaged by the storm collapsed onto the bus she was riding in.

Hurricane Irma killed at least 10 people during the 72 hours that it battered Cuba, damaged nearly every region of the island nation and left parts of Havana's picturesque historic district still underwater Monday, authorities said.

Its collision with Cuba and other Caribbean islands sapped some of its energy, possibly saving Florida from worse damage. By the time Irma made landfall on Marco Island, on the Florida peninsula, its winds had dropped from 185 mph to 130 mph. While still a massive storm — it was about 400 miles wide — Irma ended up causing less than the catastrophic damage that many had feared.

Cuba, however, was not so lucky.

The storm first hit there at 9 p.m. Friday, slamming the island's northern coast and becoming the first Category 5 hurricane to make landfall in Cuba in more than 80 years. Irma did not leave the country until Sunday afternoon.

Given the storm's immense girth, few parts of the island were spared. Even Havana, hundreds of miles from where the hurricane first struck, suffered severe flooding and wind damage, with waves up to 30 feet lashing the seaside boardwalk known as the Malecon.

Parts of Havana's colorful historic district were still flooded with chest-high water Monday, according to Cuba's state newspaper *Granma*. It called the flooding "perhaps the most severe" ever to affect Havana's coastline and said low-

A young man floats a girl on a block of styrofoam through a flooded street in Havana, after the passage of Hurricane Irma in Cuba, Sunday, Sept. 10, 2017. (AP Photo/Ramon Espinosa)

lying parts of the city were under 5 feet of water. Videos showed kitchen appliances bobbing down streets that had become rivers and residents using mattresses as boats.

The hurricane also flooded coastal areas from Baracoa, a city near the island's eastern tip still recovering from last year's Hurricane Matthew, to Matanzas in the west. Strong waves were still striking the northern coastline Monday, but were expected to subside, Cuba's weather service said.

Despite washed out roads and roofless homes, there was a sense that the storm's destruction could have been much worse.

Government officials credited the early evacuation of about 1 million people with saving lives.

The country developed a sophisticated hurricane response system in the wake of Hurricane Flora, a 1963 storm that killed 1,750 people in Cuba. The system includes standing evacuation plans for every household and frequent drills. When a big storm like Irma approaches, people whose homes are at risk are evacuated to shelters, while others move in with friends or neighbors who live in safer structures.

The National Civil Defense Council said five people were killed when their homes collapsed, including two brothers who died in Havana when a ceiling caved in and three men who failed to follow evacuation orders and died in their homes in the cities of Ciego de Avila, Camaguey and Matanzas.

In this Sunday, Sept. 10, 2017 photo, people wade through a flooded street after the passage of Hurricane Irma in Havana, Cuba. (AP Photo/Ramon Espinosa)

Ramon Pardo Guerra, chief of the National Defense Council, told the state newspaper that the damage to Cuban banana, rice and sugar cane farms was "incalculable." Nearly 1,200 square miles of sugar cane fields were destroyed, Pardo said.

In a public address later published in Granma, Cuban President Raul Castro said the storm also severely damaged the nation's electrical system as well as key tourist destinations, including Varadero, a beach resort popular with foreigners.

Castro said the government would work to make sure those areas were repaired before the busy winter season to protect the tourism industry, which has become an important part of the Communist island's economy.

"These have been difficult days for our people, who in a few hours' time have seen what was constructed with great effort hit by a devastating hurricane," Castro said.

"This is not a time to mourn," Castro said, "but to construct again that which the winds of Irma attempted to destroy."

Humans weren't the only victims.

The news site Diario de Cuba reported that hundreds of flamingos died on Cayo Coco island.

Six dolphins had better luck.

Typically housed in an aquarium on the island of Cayo Guillermo, the dolphins were airlifted by helicopter ahead of the hurricane to a salt-water pool in the south of the country and survived the storm. ∎

© 2017 Los Angeles Times

Residents walk on Havana's flooded sea wall as the ocean crashes into it, after the passing of Hurricane Irma in Havana, Cuba, Sunday, Sept. 10, 2017. (AP Photo/Ramon Espinosa)

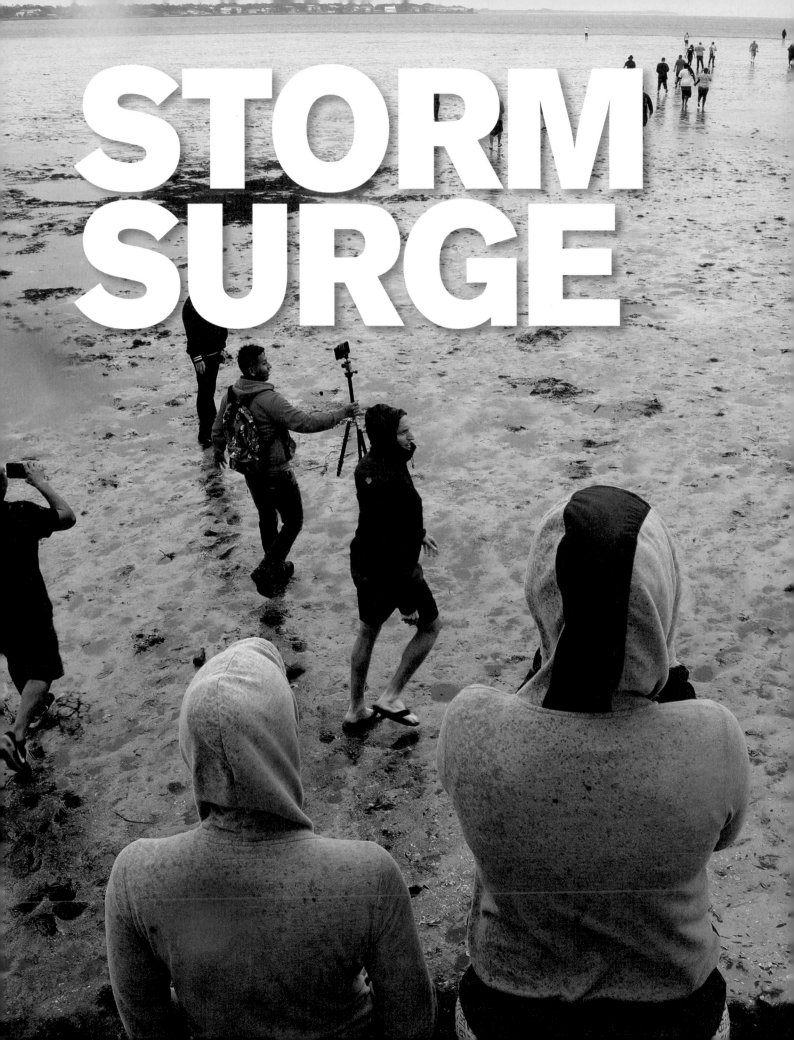

# STORM
# SURGE

# WHAT HAPPENS WHEN THE SEA RISES UP?

## Water sometimes proves more deadly than wind

By John Cherwa

*Los Angeles Times* | Tribune News Service | September 10, 2017

ORLANDO — Hurricanes are often defined and categorized by their wind speed, but the real danger comes not from furious winds but from the sudden, often fatal rise of the sea.

There is more loss of life through drowning than any other of the various deadly hazards posed by these tropical storms.

Storm surge is basically the wind blowing water toward the shore at a rate at which it overwhelms levees and seawalls designed to protect the shore. If the area close to shore is shallow, as it is in Florida, the water builds quickly and at some point overwhelms the surrounding coastal area, because it has no place else to go.

There are other factors besides geography that can make this dangerous. The size of the storm, barometric pressure and the direction the storm is coming from are factors in causing the sea to surge.

Large storms, such as Irma, are bad because water can start to build well in advance of the storm. It's as if the storm brings with it its own extra supply of water. This phenomenon is sometimes called a "bubble" or "bulge" of water.

People walking on Old Tampa Bay, in Tampa, Fla. Hurricane Irma's devastating storm surge came with weird twists that scientists attribute to the storm's girth, path and some geographic quirks. They can explain why the highest water levels observed from Irma were in faraway corners, while places closer to the eye experienced a rare reverse surge. (AP Photo/Chris O'Meara, File)

One way of thinking about it is as a tidal wave caused by wind, rather than by an earthquake or volcanic eruption.

Hurricane Katrina in 2005 was only a Category 3 storm, but it was immense in size. With a storm surge of 28 feet, combined with a broken levee, the city of New Orleans was quickly underwater. About 1,800 people lost their lives in the storm — the majority from drowning.

Most coastal communities on the Atlantic Ocean and Gulf of Mexico are no more than 10 feet above sea level, so the ability to take a big storm surge is not great. Water has only one place to go when it hits land or concrete, and that is up.

Hurricanes are cyclonic, with winds moving counterclockwise in the Northern Hemisphere. If you have a storm heading north and you are on the northeast side of the eye of the hurricane, the wind is pushing water toward the shore in advance of the storm. Once you are on the southern side of the storm, the water will recede as it is being pulled away from shore, and rather quickly it will return to normal.

It's why the real danger for the people of Naples, Fort Myers and Tampa, on the west side of the state and the storm, will come after the eye has passed. As the storm approached, water was being drawn from the shore, creating an illusion of a very low tide. As soon as the eye passes and the winds switch, the water that had receded will be blown back, as well as the reserve of water that had built up.

The storm surge in the Naples-Fort Myers area was expected to be 10 to 12 feet.

The other problem with a storm surge is that they are fast: A 10-foot storm surge at sea level can submerge the first floor of a building in a matter of minutes. ∎

© 2017 Los Angeles Times

Chris Morgan walks to the large boats on Tuesday, Sept. 12, 2017, that beached onto the property she stayed  on during Hurricane Irma's storm surge in Key Largo, Fla. (Al Diaz/Miami Herald via AP)

# DANGER LINGERS
## IN FLORIDA AS IRMA MOVES INTO GEORGIA

## Millions without power as storm makes way north

### By Evan Halper and Laura King
*Los Angeles Times* | Tribune News Service | September 11, 2017

MARCO ISLAND, Fla. — As a mighty hurricane, Irma inspired fear. As a tropical storm, it is spreading soggy distress — and continuing peril — across a growing swath of the American Southeast.

In what could be a long and messy afterlife, it will tax the patience of millions.

On Monday, a day after visiting lashing rains, surging tides and terrifying winds on nearly every corner of Florida, Irma unleashed flash flooding in three states and left a sweaty, disruptive legacy: no power for about 7 million people.

Confronting a panorama of destruction stretching from coast to coast, with rescue efforts still in progress and a massive cleanup only beginning to gather pace, Florida and federal officials opted for frankness: It might take weeks for electricity to be fully restored.

The storm's direct death toll, mercifully, was not commensurate with Irma's wrath. Authorities in Georgia on Monday reported three storm-related deaths, without providing details, and one person died in South Carolina. An electrocution was reported in central Florida — a grim hazard in flooding's aftermath. Irma is being blamed for 34 deaths in the Caribbean before it hit Florida, according to The Associated Press.

With power cut for about 6.5 million Floridians and hundreds of thousands of others in Georgia and South Carolina, restoring electricity was an urgent priority, but authorities warned that the fixes wouldn't happen overnight.

"I would caution people to be very patient here," Tom Bossert, the White House homeland security adviser, said at a briefing in Washington, D.C. "We could have power down in homes for the coming weeks."

In recorded history, the U.S. mainland had never before suffered two Category 4 hurricanes in the span of a year, never mind a little over two weeks. Coming on the heels of Hurricane Harvey's devastation in Texas, Irma was expected to be one of the country's most expensive weather disasters.

A street is flooded as Hurricane Irma passes through Naples, Fla., Sunday, Sept. 10, 2017. (AP Photo/David Goldman)

# Eleventh-hour shifts in Irma's trajectory undoubtedly saved both lives and property.

But on Monday, major insurers were revising estimates downward, though they were still expected to run in the tens of billions of dollars.

Still, as the storm left Florida behind, the danger lingered: Storm surges jeopardized cities along the state's Gulf and Atlantic coasts, and the National Hurricane Center said Irma was still spinning off 60-mph winds as it moved into Georgia on Monday afternoon.

In Jacksonville, Fla., water poured rapidly into downtown streets, with the St. Johns River hitting flood levels not seen in decades.

"Get out NOW," the Jacksonville Sheriff's Office tweeted in a warning to people in evacuation zones. It advised those who needed help escaping flooded homes to visibly display something white — a shirt or a pillowcase.

Downtown Charleston, S.C., too was hit by heavy storm flooding, and communities in coastal Georgia were swamped as well.

With Irma's reach spreading over hundreds of miles, Alabama battened down; schools and businesses closed across the state. In Georgia, Hartsfield-Jackson Atlanta International Airport was still open Monday, but thousands of flights have been canceled.

Although the storm's raging winds and punishing rains lent it an apocalyptic feel as it unfolded in Florida over the weekend, damage initially appeared significant and widespread, but short of catastrophic.

That was true even in the Florida Keys, where Irma made landfall as a Category 4 hurricane. Florida Gov. Rick Scott, who flew in with the Coast Guard plane, said he saw "devastation" — roofs ripped away, boats tossed ashore, mobile homes overturned — but "it's not as bad as we thought."

Still he cautioned, "It's going to be a long road; there's a lot of damage."

Eleventh-hour shifts in Irma's trajectory undoubtedly saved both lives and property. Last week, while the storm was roaring through the Caribbean, where it devastated a chain of small islands, one projected track had it aiming straight for Miami, Florida's biggest city. But it veered westward instead.

On Sunday, still at hurricane strength, Irma appeared set for a direct strike on the highly built-up Gulf Coast region of Tampa-St. Petersburg, but it tacked east-northeast instead, losing strength as it moved over land.

Experts say the number of deaths and amount of damage that can be expected from a storm of that strength have been reduced in recent years by advances in forecasting, which enable authorities to order people out of harm's way, and stricter building standards that help fortify the sorts of large public venues where people seek shelter — even if smaller wooden structures remain vulnerable.

While the seas to Florida's west bent to Irma's will, receding and then rising, the National Hurricane Center also warned of "significant river flooding" for the next five days along the storm track. Scott called that flood threat the storm's most dangerous aftermath.

On Monday, just outside Orlando, hundreds of homes were ordered emptied as floodwaters rose, and firefighters staged boat rescues for some. Another classic Florida hazard struck nearby: A 60-foot sinkhole abruptly gaped at the base of an apartment building, which was hastily evacuated. No injuries were reported.

Not all damage has yet been chronicled. Except for rescuers and suppliers, the Florida Keys were mainly unreachable by the single 42-bridge highway linking them, although a flotilla of boats was making its way.

The Navy said it was sending in four vessels, including the aircraft carrier Lincoln, to provide emergency services in the Keys.

Coast Guard and naval helicopters buzzed over the low-lying island chain, making aerial assessments. Units of the Florida National Guard and other personnel were deployed for the cleanup, bringing bulldozers and other heavy equipment with them.

In Florida City, the gateway to the Keys, frustration mounted among those who wanted to go back home after obeying orders to get out.

"I'm sorry I ever agreed to evacuate," said Warren Stincer, a boat captain and carpenter from Key Largo. "My home is just 20 minutes down the road, and I know the road is clear."

Joe Sanchez, spokesman for the Florida Highway Patrol, said the road would remain closed to all but emergency crews until authorities determined it was safe.

President Donald Trump expressed resolve in the face of the twin hurricanes, even if his administration is skeptical of climate changes that scientists say are contributing to increasingly violent weather.

At a Pentagon ceremony commemorating the Sept. 11 attacks of 16 years ago, Trump pledged

Tommy Nevitt carries Miranda Abbott, 6, through floodwater caused by Hurricane Irma on the west side of Jacksonville, Fla., Monday, Sept. 11 2017. (Dede Smith/The Florida Times-Union via AP)

support for those afflicted by the storms in Florida and Texas.

"These are storms of catastrophic severity, and we are marshaling the full resources of the federal government to help our fellow Americans," the president said.

As Monday dawned, many people headed out to check on damage despite officials' warnings of continued hazards, including high waters, downed power lines and sewage-tainted floodwaters.

At the Riverwood Estates mobile home park in Naples, on the Gulf Coast, Terry Thompson, 65, was among those surveying what the storm had wrought. He rode out the storm with his dog in his mobile home, which he'd moved into only two weeks earlier.

His neighbor's carport roof had flown off and smacked into his wife's car, and tree branches and debris littered the streets of the complex.

"There's a lot of cleanup," he said. But his car and boat were intact.

After making landfall early Sunday in the Keys, the storm spent Sunday chewing and churning its way up much of the Gulf Coast, but also paralyzing Miami, the normally buzzing metropolis on the other side of the peninsula. Most people were trapped indoors all day by wind and rain while floodwaters rose in downtown streets.

On Monday, the city looked bedraggled, but the sun was shining. Still, authorities were asking people to stay indoors, and many businesses remained shuttered.

Miami International Airport, the scene of a frantic exodus in the days before the storm struck, said it would be closed Monday, with limited flights beginning Tuesday. Hundreds of flights were canceled over the weekend. The airport's director, Emilio Gonzalez, tweeted that the airport, hit by gusts of nearly 100 mph, "sustained significant water damage throughout." ■

*Halper reported from Marco Island and King from Washington.* Times *staff writers Patrick McConnell in Florida City and John Cherwa in Orlando contributed to this report.*

© 2017 Los Angeles Times

A vehicle drives on flooded Brickell Avenue in Miami on Sunday, Sept. 10, 2017, as Hurricane Irma passes. (Mike Stocker/South Florida Sun-Sentinel via AP)

# FLOODING INCREASES
## IN CENTRAL FLORIDA AS POWER IS RESTORED FOR THOUSANDS MORE

### Rising water levels remain a danger

By Stephen Hudak

*Orlando Sentinel* | Tribune News Service | September 12, 2017

ORLANDO — Surging waters spawned by Hurricane Irma's heavy rains caused flooding in several parts of Central Florida on Tuesday, even as power was slowly being restored and the massive cleanup effort began.

About 400 people, including nursing home residents with special needs, were evacuated Tuesday from Good Samaritan Society's flood-prone Kissimmee Village. The 425-acre gated retirement community south of Kissimmee flooded at the highest level ever, county officials said.

"Many of the people here are not just over the age of 55 but over 80," said Good Samaritan resident Lynne VonEsch, 76, who was pacing the parking lot of a shelter Tuesday with Marnie, her 7-year-old Goldendoodle, a therapy dog.

Rising waters also threatened neighborhoods along the Little Wekiva River in Seminole County, in Apopka, in eastern Lake County and near the University of Central Florida.

Flooding from the Little Wekiva forced the evacuation of 61 people and 18 pets from Spring Oaks, an Altamonte Springs subdivision just north of State Road 436. Evacuees were taken to shelters.

Altamonte Springs City Manager Frank Martz said the city would "assess the stability" of homes after the water recedes. He was not sure when that would be.

About 90 homes in the Oaks of Wekiva were in danger of flooding because of an overflowing retention pond, Apopka Mayor Joe Kilsheimer said.

"You've got a whole subdivision of people watching the steadily rising water," Kilsheimer said.

A sign outside a home where a family rode out Hurricane Irma is shown, Tuesday, Sept. 12, 2017, in Key Largo, Fla., in the Florida Keys. (AP Photo/Wilfredo Lee)

Some residents at The Place, an apartment complex on Alafaya Trail near UCF, reported water in their units.

Sheila Bonnough, 23, who had fled to her parents' home in Melbourne, was alerted by a friend to flooding that ruined her furniture.

"When he left it was up to his ankles," she said.

The owners of Wekiva Island closed the entertainment complex on the river's southern edge amid fears of flooding.

"The water is knee deep throughout the park," said Mary Sue Weinaug, whose husband owns the venue. "We now have 5 acres of river flowing through our property."

The National Weather Service issued a flood warning for the rural community of Astor in eastern Lake County.

"Astor flood waters have reached levels never seen before," county spokeswoman Elisha Pappacoda said.

County officials urged residents in Astor and nearby Lake George to evacuate, imposed a curfew from 9 p.m. to 7:30 a.m. in the area, and began enforcing a "No Wake Zone" on the St. Johns River.

Although most shelters in Central Florida closed, some evacuees who sought refuge from Irma could not go home.

Some homes were deemed no longer fit to live in and others were still without power late Tuesday.

An auditorium at a Longwood mega-church — Northland, a Church Distributed — became a temporary haven for evacuees who had been staying at Red Cross-run shelters.

Among the 150 people at the Northland, Marvelene Kooistra, 95, was persuaded by her Maitland neighbors to go to the church rather than back home.

"I told them, 'I can live in my house with no air conditioning. I can eat out of a can,'" she said. "But I was outvoted."

Residents across Central Florida started the massive cleanup of knocked-down trees, fences and pool enclosures, while hundreds of thousands of people waited to be reconnected to the region's power grid more than 40 hours after Irma.

Cynthia Gorel, who spent Tuesday picking up twigs and other storm debris in a dress, said she was tired of the post-Irma diet of peanut butter and jelly sandwiches. The Winter Park woman also said she longed for an air-conditioned room and a hot shower.

"I may try to find a hotel tonight," she said.

But many others got power back, a signal that life in Central Florida is slowly returning to normal.

More and more grocery stores, restaurants and other businesses reopened.

Melissa Newton of Winter Springs took her 5-year-old son Dylan to Aloma Bowl to blow off energy.

"He's been cooped up in the house for days," she said as he lobbed an orange ball that bounced then rolled into a gutter.

Dozens had the same idea.

"We've been getting calls all day," said Jennifer Halpern, the bowling alley manager.

She said most callers asked two questions: Do you have air conditioning and can we charge our phones there?

The storm, blamed for 12 deaths in Florida, also may cost Orlando International Airport as much as $20 million, according to an early estimate by Phil Brown, executive director for the Greater Orlando Aviation Authority.

He said the airport suffered substantial storm damage, including some from flooding. A JetBlue hangar lost its roof and contractors had to repair broken jet bridges, clear waterlogged parking areas and remove debris prior to flights resuming Tuesday.

"We expect, over the next several days, the airlines are going to ramp up to full service," Brown said. ∎

*Staff writers Martin E. Comas, Ryan Gillespie, Bianca Padro Ocasio, Jason Ruiter, Kate Santich and Jeffrey Weiner contributed to this story*

Debbie McCulley walks her bike through the flooded Brookside Avenue in Kissimmee, Fla. on Sept. 11, 2017, as Brian Rondon and his dog Zeus also check out the new waterway. (Jacob Langston/Orlando Sentinel/TNS)

Bruce Gee, 11, walks his dog Sarge through the trailer park on Marathon Key, in the Florida Keys, where a surge from Hurricane Irma swept through the park and damaged their home, September 11, 2017. (Charles Trainor Jr./Miami Herald via AP)

# PART 3
# THE
# AFTERMATH

# "BASICALLY EVERY HOUSE" IN FLORIDA KEYS AFFECTED

## Some residents allowed back to survey damage

By Evan Halper and Laura King
Tribune Washington Bureau | Tribune News Service | September 12, 2017

JACKSONVILLE — Residents of the hurricane-hammered Florida Keys began returning home Tuesday to a primitive, pared-down version of their former lives, with most lacking basic necessities such as electricity, water, sanitation systems or cellphone service.

The woes spawned by former Hurricane Irma stretched from the Keys, off Florida's southern tip, to the state's far north, where the city of Jacksonville was cleaning up after its heaviest flooding in decades and coping with a continuing high-water threat.

David and Dee Thorne hug near the remains of their home following Hurricane Irma on Big Pine Key in the Florida Keys, on September 20, 2017. They are living in an RV on the lot as they begin to repair the house. (Charles Trainor Jr./Miami Herald/TNS)

# The neighborhood suffered a 12-hour outage, and the road near his house was partially closed by a sparking transformer — a microcosm of the power woes statewide.

The Jacksonville sheriff's office said more than 350 people had been plucked to safety from floodwaters, and warned people to take heed of any further evacuation orders.

"There are so many areas you'd never have thought would have flooded, that flooded," said Gov. Rick Scott, who visited Jacksonville on Tuesday. "Thank God everybody helped everybody here."

Across the state, millions struggled to cope with power outages, fuel shortages and a massive cleanup that was still in its earliest stages. President Donald Trump planned to visit the hurricane zone Thursday, the White House said without disclosing an itinerary.

Despite causing such widespread damage, Irma was blamed for relatively few fatalities on the U.S. mainland, after killing at least 36 people on its rampage through the eastern Caribbean last week.

There have been seven storm-related deaths in Florida, four in South Carolina and two in Georgia, according to The Associated Press, but officials have questioned whether some of those fatalities can be directly attributed to Irma.

Florida's storm-imposed isolation was easing. Although gasoline was still hard to come by in much of the state, frustrating motorists, Miami International Airport reported that it was gradually resuming service Tuesday but advised people to check with airlines to make sure their flights were actually scheduled.

The storm's lingering winds were snarling air traffic as far away as Atlanta, where hundreds of flights were canceled Tuesday at Hartsfield-Jackson airport, the world's busiest in terms of passenger traffic, where gusts up to 64 mph were reported.

In Florida, the port of Tampa reopened Tuesday afternoon to big ships, which will allow fuel tankers to make much-needed deliveries.

With the remnants of the once-powerful hurricane dumping rain as it dissipated over a broad swath of the Southeast, including Georgia, Alabama and South Carolina, an army of work crews was mobilized to try to restore electricity, which was cut for nearly three-quarters of Florida's homes and businesses, crippling commercial activity and hampering recovery efforts.

The electricity cutoffs affected 15 million people, Christopher Krebs, an assistant secretary in the Department of Homeland Security, said at a briefing in Washington on Tuesday — a figure extrapolated from utilities' reports that nearly 6 million customers had lost power, with each account representing more than one person.

Other estimates were lower, in the neighborhood of 10 million affected, and the numbers were fluctuating as some repairs were carried out more quickly than others. Utility crews were working around the clock, officials said, including an additional 30,000 workers from out of state, the governor told reporters.

Some progress was being reported, though. Florida Power and Light said it hoped to have service restored to many of its customers on the Atlantic coast in the next five days, although damage was worse — and will take longer to fix — on the Gulf of Mexico side. In South Carolina, utility officials reported progress in halving the number of outages from a peak of about 250,000 customers.

In other signs of nascent normality, curfews were being lifted in storm-stricken Florida cities and cruise-ship passengers were disembarking after voyages extended by the storm.

"We've got a lot of work to do, but everybody's going to come together and get this state rebuilt," Scott said.

The peninsula's major population centers on the Gulf and Atlantic coasts, including Miami in the east and Tampa-St. Petersburg in the west, suffered considerably less damage than feared as the storm's track veered away from them.

But parts of the Keys, a fragile archipelago linked to the mainland by a single roadway and 42 bridges, faced a longer road to recovery. Only in the less severely impacted upper Keys, closest to the mainland, were evacuees being allowed to return.

The head of the Federal Emergency Management Agency, William B. "Brock" Long, said Tuesday that by initial estimates, a quarter of the homes in the Keys were destroyed and an additional 60 percent damaged. In all, "basically every house in the Keys was impacted," he said.

One of those who chose to ride out the hurricane in Key West was 90-year-old Shirley Ross Block. Speaking by phone, she recounted her fears during the storm that roofs might fly off — including hers — but they held, she said.

Block initially thought the evacuation order wasn't necessary, but changed her mind when confronted with the aftermath: power outage, rationed running water and dwindling propane for generators. If everyone had stayed, she said, "there would be all the more people in dire straits now."

Much of the recovery work in the Keys so far has simply been fixing washed-out roads and preparing landing strips for emergency-response flights. Planes are able to land now at two airports in the island chain, in Key West and Marathon, said officials in Monroe County, which encompasses the Keys.

All three of the archipelago's hospitals were shuttered, but officials hoped to reopen at least one, in Tavernier, soon, and food-distribution points and shelters were being set up at locales including Key West and Cudjoe Key, where the hurricane made landfall on Sunday.

The aircraft carrier Lincoln was dispatched to waters close to Key West to aid in the rescue effort in the islands.

Four hundred miles to the north in Jacksonville, the stench of wastewater hung in the air, and city officials were busy cleaning up debris left by the receded floodwaters. In the Talleyrand neighborhood, Eugene Hawkins' home stayed dry, but neighbors on lower ground were hit by flooding.

Hawkins, 40, lives close to a power plant, and as a result, rarely loses electricity in storms, he said. This time, though, the neighborhood suffered a 12-hour outage, and the road near his house was partially closed by a sparking transformer — a microcosm of the power woes statewide.

Maj. Gen. Michael Calhoun, Florida's adjutant general, said there were 8,000 members of the Florida National Guard on the ground and 16 aircraft in the air, pushing ahead with search and rescue where needed and recovery elsewhere.

After Irma came to life last week as one of the most powerful Atlantic hurricanes recorded, the storm's worst fury was reserved for a string of Caribbean islands, many of them territories of France, Britain and the Netherlands.

French President Emmanuel Macron and Dutch King Willem-Alexander were in the devastated area Tuesday, with British Foreign Secretary Boris Johnson expected as well — all of them offering support but fending off angry accusations of a less-than-robust initial response to the disaster. ∎

*Halper reported from Jacksonville and King from Washington.* Times *staff writer Molly Hennessy-Fiske in Houston contributed to this report.*

© 2017 Tribune Washington Bureau

Mirta Mendez walks through debris at the Seabreeze trailer park along the Overseas Highway in the Florida Keys. When Hurricane Irma slammed into the Lower Florida Keys, it destroyed or severely damaged nearly all of the area's mobile homes where many of its service industry workers live. Business owners and county leaders are racing to secure temporary housing for those workers while trying to preserve the island chain's small-town, mom-and-pop atmosphere. (Al Diaz/Miami Herald via AP, File)

# AN **EXASPERATING HUNT** FOR GASOLINE

## Many stymied in effort to return home

By Evan Halper

Tribune Washington Bureau | Tribune News Service | September 12, 2017

GAINESVILLE — The drive from Naples to Gainesville was 288 miles of gut-wrenching anxiety, and not because of destruction from the massive hurricane that tore through the day before.

Along that entire stretch of Interstate 75 — four hours from far southwest Florida to nearly the top of the state — there was hardly a functioning gas pump to be found.

Mile after mile, motorists were exiting the freeway on fumes and encountering the same sorry sight: empty gas pumps covered with yellow bags, or even worse, wrapped in the dreaded shrink wrap.

"We are just trying to get back," said Rachel Monteagudo, who was hauling an oversized camper from Georgia back to Fort Lauderdale after fleeing the storm — but hadn't seen any gas since she'd crossed the state line.

Hurricane Irma threw Florida into an epic gas crisis, turning the minor chore of filling up into what could feel like a fool's errand. With ships unable to make deliveries through the storm and power outages forcing stations to close, up to 40 percent of the gas stations in the state were unable to provide fuel Tuesday, the online source GasBuddy reported.

As hundreds of thousands of evacuated Floridians motor back toward homes in areas ravaged by the hurricane, the hunt for gas has become a communal obsession.

People loiter at empty gas stations in the hope the situation might change. A car drives into an empty station and parks; soon a dozen more cars pile in, thinking the driver knew something they didn't.

This happened at a Thornton's filling station north of Tampa. An empty parking lot quickly came alive with chattering motorists hoping for gas. One motorist started pouring gas into her tank from big plastic containers. Nearby, a man had been snoozing in a jalopy he had aspirationally parked alongside a shuttered pump. Now he got out and approached the woman, wanting to know where she'd gotten the gas.

It turned out it had been pumped days before, at a station hundreds of miles away.

Frederick Wilson, 66, had to drive 30 miles from his home in Georgetown, Fla., to find gasoline, on I-95, to run his generator. His house has no power and he lost the roof. (Carolyn Cole/Los Angeles Times/TNS)

Some state ports where gas normally gets distributed are just now reopening. Regular gas refineries and supply lines disrupted by the wreckage Hurricane Harvey wrought last month in Texas are still recovering. And gas trucks were blocked for days making their way down the Florida coast as Irma passed through.

It all created a desperate situation up and down the state.

The one station that appeared to be open off I-75 north of Tampa on Monday night created chaos. A line down the exit ramp extended miles up the highway. Police lights glared by the intersection, with stressed officers trying to bring some order to the hordes of desperate drivers gridlocked at the filling station entrance.

The appearance of the gas line caused others to stop, setting off a chain reaction down the already clogged highway and bringing traffic to a near standstill for at least 15 miles.

Environmentalists have weighed in on TV, blaming the state's heavy dependence on oil and pointing to how much less gas everyone would need had there been more hybrids on Florida interstates and fewer fuel-guzzling SUVs. SUV enthusiasts blamed environmentalists, complaining that their hostility to new oil pipelines worsened the shortages that choked Florida.

Often, motorists blamed one another.

When a couple of retirement age pulled up to a pump in Gainesville, they shot a look of incredulity and annoyance at a journalist who informed them there wasn't a drop of gas in the station — or pretty much any station for the next 250 miles.

"I don't believe what you are saying," the man huffed, signaling his intention to get back in the car with its nearly empty tank and keep heading toward Venice, some 200 miles away. All he needed to do was get a few miles off the interstate, he insisted, and he would find something.

His companion's face went pale.

Stocking up on gas has become so advisable that even gas cans are hard to come by. One station owner charged $66 for three empty plastic gas containers. A police officer watched as he rang up the sale.

"How do you live with yourself?" he asked the owner.

Gainesville was the most fuel-parched city in the state, according to GasBuddy, making it probably the most parched place in America, though it wasn't clear why: The city made it through the storm in far better shape than other places that seemed to have more gas.

At one empty station in town, sheriff's deputies in several squad cars congregated at an apparently empty gas station. Asked by a reporter why they were loitering at a gas station with no gas, one of the officers responded warily. "I have nothing to say about that," he said.

Nearby, Devontshe Care sat in his car by one of the empty pumps, looking forlorn. The Key West resident trying to get home figured he had enough fuel to make it maybe 50 miles. He had a lot farther than that to go. He had seen some open stations pumping gas farther north, but the lines were long. He'd kept driving.

"I kept thinking, it'll get a little better if I keep going," he said. "It didn't get better. Now I don't know when I am going to make it back." Care, a candy store manager, fiddled with his phone, looking for recent reports of gas nearby. There were none.

Gas was trickling back into the state by Tuesday, though even then, it took unwavering determination to get any of it.

Frederick Wilson, 66, set out on a desperate search near Georgetown, where the storm had wrecked the roof of his home and knocked out electricity. A borrowed generator kept the refrigerator running and emergency cellphones charged.

But the generator was out of gas. Wilson's car was not far behind. Every gas station he went to was closed. He drove five miles, then 10. Nothing. At 15 miles, he said, "I got into a gas line, circa the 1970s," referring to the long waits during the energy crisis of that decade. "I got up to the third in line. Then they ran out."

He drove nervously on, his gas needle dropping.

In Gainesville, Fla., along I-75, gasoline is very hard to find on Tuesday, Sept. 12, 2017. Devontshe Care sits in the driver's seat of his car by one of the empty pumps, looking forlorn. The Key West resident, trying to get home, figured he had enough fuel to make it maybe 50 miles. He had a lot further than that to go. (Carolyn Cole/Los Angeles Times/TNS)

Then, bingo: He saw a gas tanker pulled up at a station, and a fellow driver said fuel was about to flow. Wilson eagerly lined his own car up at the pump.

Presently, the driver of the tanker emerged from the convenience store, hopped in his cab and drove away. He didn't have gas. He'd stopped for snacks.

Wilson finally found fuel at a Flying J off I-95, another 15 miles away. "Now I have to drive 30 miles back to my house," he said.

Soon, he'd need more gas. ∎

© 2017 Tribune Washington Bureau

# Destruction along the northern swath of the Keys

### By Patrick J. McDonnell
*Los Angeles Times* | Tribune News Service
September 12, 2017

ISLAMORADA, Fla. — People here like to throw around the word "paradise," but these days Route 1 down the spine of the Florida Keys cuts through a jagged tableau of destruction.

Felled palms, splintered trailers and homes, and piles of trash — boats, furniture, appliances and other assorted debris — line the roadside, testament to the force of Hurricane Irma as it careened through the islands.

Shuttered doors and tangles of broken branches conceal resorts with resonant names such as Kon-Tiki, the Banyan Tree, La Siesta and the Green Turtle Inn.

Many residents were returning to their homes Tuesday for the first time, as police allowed access to the northern swath of the Keys. Many expected the worst, and that is what they found amid rubble that glistened beneath an unforgiving tropical sun.

"I moved here because I wanted paradise — and I got it, at least for a month," said Laura

Mike Gilbert and his daughter, Brook Gilbert, 15, stand over the remnants of a three-story, 12-unit condominium near Islamorada, along the Overseas Highway in the Florida Keys, on Tuesday, Sept. 12, 2017. Mike Gilbert was a resident in the building, which collapsed during the storm surge caused by Hurricane Irma. (Al Diaz/Miami Herald/TNS)

Costello, 52, a former South Pasadena, Calif., resident who was found walking through the ruins of the Sea Breeze trailer park in Islamorada, a few miles south of Key Largo.

The Keys had perhaps taken the heaviest blow from Irma — federal authorities estimated that 85 percent of the homes were damaged or destroyed — but the storm left its muddy footprints all over Florida and into Alabama, Georgia and South Carolina. It was still plodding north on Tuesday, spreading rain over a widening swath of the Southeast. In its wake was a massive cleanup job, complicated by fuel shortages and power outages; an estimated 15 million people in the Southeast lacked electricity.

In Florida, there was significant damage as far north as Jacksonville, which sustained its heaviest flooding in decades.

President Donald Trump planned to visit the hurricane zone Thursday, the White House said, without disclosing an itinerary.

The death toll from the storm was rising, with 12 fatalities in Florida, four in South Carolina and two in Georgia, according to The Associated Press. The storm killed at least 36 people on its rampage through the eastern Caribbean last week before hitting Florida with full force on Sunday.

By Tuesday, Islamorada looked like a malevolent giant had come stomping through, wreaking havoc on people's homes and personal possessions. Gnarled chunks of aluminum siding were thrown about with wood beams, many with protruding nails, and other pieces of former residences.

Among the many nautical remnants: a placard found tossed in the pearl-white sand of the trailer park that declared: "To our guests. Thou shalt not bring thy worries aboard."

A few American flags fluttered from the wreckage.

Costello said she began renting a trailer here a month ago for $1,500 a month. She always loved the sea.

"This was the ultimate for me," she said. "I could sit out and watch the sun rise and set. It was what I always wanted. It was a dream."

Her one-bedroom trailer is now a ragged wreck, pushed 10 yards off its cement foundation. Her seaside deck was blown 15 yards away.

"There's my bed," Costello said, pointing at a wooden frame half a block from where her home was. "Those are my curtains."

Fortunately, she heeded the warnings and evacuated last Wednesday with her most precious possessions. She had lived in Florida for more than 20 years and didn't discount the dangers of hurricanes.

On Tuesday she plucked from the ruins of her dream home a single item: a glass frame mounted with color photographs of her three children when they were young. All are grown now.

"I have my health, I have my life, I'm fine," said Costello, a bartender in nearby Key Largo, standing at the splintered entrance to her trailer. "I'm just glad I got out of here."

Nearby were storefronts with plywood strips and shattered windows — and in some cases blown-off roofs. There were storm-battered wine bars, cafes, fish joints, yoga haunts and bait shops. Piled junk obscured the colorful mural of a mermaid on a motel wall.

The trail of damage seemed oddly disjointed. Destroyed homes sat next to other structures that appeared largely unaffected.

In a small harbor, several manatees came to the surface to drink fresh water from a faucet dripping into a now becalmed sea. The slow-moving sea mammals maneuvered around a sunken fishing boat.

But many storage facilities where people kept their vessels onshore seemed to have escaped major harm.

The damage was reported to be even more severe to the south in Marathon, but police closed access. Several small planes at the airport there were reportedly flipped over, and authorities endeavored to clear debris-choked streets.

Here in Islamorada, the Gilbert family was contemplating the remains of their condo, once on the third floor of a 12-unit complex along Route 1. The land is very narrow here, perhaps a quarter of a mile or less across, and the sea appeared to have ripped straight through the condominium complex. Most of it sank into the soft sand.

The three-story structure had pancaked, leaving the family's third-level condo at ground level, in front of a pool of water with ripped pipes and other debris.

Homes leveled by Hurricane Irma on Big Pine Key, Fla., Sept. 13, 2017. (Rob O'Neal /The Key West Citizen via AP)

"This is very emotional for me and my family," said Brooke Gilbert, 15, gazing at the remains of the structure and showing a visitor a cellphone snapshot of the building in better times.

The family drove down Tuesday from their home in Fort Lauderdale to view the damage. The condo was her grandparents', but had been part of the Gilberts' life for many years. Someone had sent them a photo of the destroyed structure, but they only arrived Tuesday to view it firsthand. They were in collective disbelief.

"This is where I learned to swim, where I learned to drive a boat, where I caught my first lobster," said Brooke, holding back tears as she and her father, Michael Gilbert, observed their smashed home.

It was too unsteady to go inside to retrieve personal items.

"It's just very difficult for us to come back here and see this," said Brooke. "It was such a part of all of our lives. Now it's gone." ∎

*Staff writers Evan Halper in Jacksonville, Fla., and Laura King in Washington contributed to this report.*

Tom Ross inspects the damage to his three-story condominium building in the aftermath of Hurricane Irma in Islamorada, Fla., on Tuesday, Sept. 12, 2017. (Marcus Yam/ Los Angeles Times/TNS)

# MIGRANT WORKERS HIT HARD BY IRMA

## These workers earn $350 a week. Now Irma has destroyed their homes.

By Patrick J. McDonnell

*Los Angeles Times* | Tribune News Service | September 12, 2017

IMMOKALEE, Fla. — Petrona Nunez cradled her 2-year-old daughter, Jazabell, in her arms and surveyed the damage to her family trailer.

The roof had caved in on the living room and bedroom. Debris was everywhere. Globs of pink insulation clung to furniture, walls and the floor, as did mudlike dollops of saturated roofing material.

A broken mirror and shattered door lay atop her bed. A plastic sheet served as a temporary roof, creating a diaphanous glow amid the chaos inside.

"It's so bad," Nunez, 24, said, clearly at a loss for words. "It's pretty sad when your home is destroyed."

In this Sept. 12, 2017 photo, Nicolas Perez keeps a puppy he named "Irma," stuffed in his shirt, who he rescued from flooding in the aftermath of Hurricane Irma, in Immokalee, Fla. The town is one of the poorest in the state. (AP Photo/Gerald Herbert)

# Roofs were blown off many of the trailer homes and ill-constructed shacks that pass as housing here for the multitudes of farmworkers, mostly from Central America and Mexico.

Hurricane Irma caused large-scale damage on its rampage through Florida, but this impoverished, largely Latino farming hub in the southwestern part of the state was among the areas hardest hit. While aid was being rushed to the Florida Keys and other ravaged coastal zones, as of Monday evening there was no sign of any help arriving to this rural backwater a day after the storm blasted through.

Immokalee — the name is said to derive from a Seminole word referring to "home" — is a place apart in Florida, remote and well off the tourist trail. Its poverty rate is among the state's highest, encompassing more than one-third of the town's 25,000 or so residents — yet it is only 50 miles or so from seaside Naples, one of the state's wealthiest communities and the hub of Collier County, which includes Immokalee.

"We're part of Florida, we're part of Collier County, but sometimes it doesn't feel like it," said Connie Velasquez, 22, a beauty parlor worker and lifelong Immokalee resident. "We're usually the last to get help."

Plywood boards mounted as protection from the storm still covered windows of the taco shops, Mexican-style grocery stores and other establishments along Main Street. There was no electricity; power lines were down on streets and in yards. Residents lined up at a generator rigged with extension cords to charge their phones.

Roofs were blown off many of the trailer homes and ill-constructed shacks that pass as housing here for the multitudes of farmworkers, mostly from Central America and Mexico, but with a considerable contingent from Haiti. Pools of water from the hurricane still were found on streets and front yards.

"I don't know who is going to fix this," said Felipe Bartolo, 59, a native of Guatemala whose rented, one-room home had its tin roof sheared off.

He pays $70 a week rent for the claustrophobic accommodation, plus an $8-a-week surcharge to run the air conditioner, vital in this sweltering, swampy enclave. On a good day, he said, he earns about $70 picking tomatoes or doing other agricultural jobs in a region that provides much of the U.S. winter tomato crop.

"The water came in, everything was soaked," said Bartolo, who, along with much of the town, was out cutting huge branches that littered front yards, roofs and sidewalks. "No one helped us."

Despite considerable property damage, there were no reported serious injuries as Irma swept through town. Most people appeared to have taken refuge in shelters set up in schools and other buildings — despite widespread fears that using such facilities could expose immigrants in the country illegally to arrest and deportation.

"A lot of people here were afraid to go to the shelters," Velasquez said. "Finally they realized they wouldn't get deported and they went. That probably saved lives."

Immokalee achieved notoriety in 1960 when it was featured in the seminal CBS documentary "Harvest of Shame," by Edward R. Murrow, which exposed the exploitation of migrant workers. Immokalee periodically hits the news in contemporary accounts of sub-minimum-wage salaries for farmworkers, slavelike conditions and other labor violations. It's not clear that the situation has improved for farmworkers here since Murrow's expose.

The feeling is very Third World: Chickens wander about the streets, and most everyone sits outside in the evening to escape the heat, although there is not a lot to do. Spanish is the prevalent language. Strangers are eyed warily. On Monday, the entire town seemed to ignore what residents said was a 5:30 p.m. police curfew following Irma's rampage.

Irma essentially worsened — and in some cases finished off — what was already a dilapidated housing stock, which includes tree-shrouded parks with aging trailers and barracks-type apartments and houses erected years ago for migrant laborers. Parts of the town resemble a 1960s, B-movie set.

The agricultural belt here was created from drained swamps. A reserve for the endangered Florida panther is situated along nearby State Road 29, which features yellow "Panther crossing" signs, with the big cat's outline. The main east-west drag, Interstate 75, is known as Alligator Alley.

Few government officials have arrived to assess the damage, residents said. There was widespread confusion about who can provide help. Cellphone coverage has been out, complicating matters.

"I thought you guys were with the Red Cross," said Jerry Thomas, 40, who is among a remnant African-American population here. "I'm looking for some help. My sister was supposed to call the Red Cross. You know anything about contacting FEMA?" he added, referring to the Federal Emergency Management Agency.

Thomas, shirtless and glistening with sweat, was using a machete to pick apart a giant mango tree that had fallen in his front yard. Its roots had lifted up his father's 1992 Saturn sedan, which had been parked out front. Thomas hunkered inside his home as the storm raged.

"It was no big deal, just the wind and rain, but then I heard, boom! It was the tree going down," Thomas said.

Two pine trees also tumbled onto his driveway, damaging his cars, a 1992 Mercedes sedan and a 2003 Ford Explorer. The branches completely covered the vehicles. But no one was hurt.

"I can only get so much done with this," he added, referring to the machete. "I need someone with a chain saw to give me a hand."

Across from his house is another wounded trailer park. The worst-hit trailer belonged to Alice Barber.

"This is my bedroom," said Barber, 59, standing next to a soaked queen mattress amid a pile of drenched sheets, pillows, towels and household items. The roof had been torn off. A line of ants marched along the floor, attacking Barber's feet.

As the storm closed in on Sunday, she gathered her valuables and moved to an apartment in a cellblock-like set of flats next to her trailer. She now lives in an apartment alongside her mother, Louise Lee, 86, who greets visitors with a warm "hello." She brought her mom down here years ago to help her out, Barber said.

"I hope FEMA comes around," said Barber, who says she survives on a monthly disability check and food stamps. "But at least we all survived. And I have my mom."

She wasn't worried about looters.

"They can take whatever they want, they already robbed the fan," Barber said. "It was all wet anyway. But we need someone to come help us out. I have to take care of my mom — and my babies."

The latter are gaggles of cats, including sundry kittens, that gather around her destroyed home. She opened a can of cat food, prompting more tiny felines to emerge from the muddy mire beneath the trailer.

"I love it here," said Barber, a native of Pennsylvania who said she initially went on the migrant trail with a "Mexican boyfriend" and settled in Immokalee more than 20 years ago. She speaks some rough Spanish. "But we need help, we need FEMA. You have any idea how to reach them?" ∎

© 2017 Los Angeles Times

In this Sept. 11, 2017 file photo, Quintana and Liz Perez look at the flooding outside their home in the aftermath of Hurricane Irma, in Immokalee, Fla, one of the poorest towns in the state. Home of many day laborers and migrant workers, Immokalee sustained heavy damage from Irma that will take months to overcome. (AP Photo/Gerald Herbert)

# BLACK CREEK RESIDENTS WON'T SURRENDER TO NATURE

## Waterway gets in their blood

By Teresa Stepzinski

*The Florida Times-Union* | Tribune News Service | September 22, 2017

MIDDLEBURG — Hurricane Irma destroyed their Black Creek home and tore apart their dream of opening their own restaurant.

"Yeah, we lost everything. But my wife is safe, we're going to have a baby. We're all safe. What do we need?" asked Dennis De St Jeor as he and his wife, Ana, walked Tuesday through the ruins of their Black Creek Drive home of five years.

Awaiting the birth of their first child, the couple said the close-knit community rallied to help them.

The raging storm surge fueled by heavy Hurricane Irma rains sent record flood waters pouring over the creek's banks, destroying homes, splintering boat houses and docks, sweeping away family treasures and shattering the lives of longtime residents and newcomers.

Middleburg resident Emmett Kesler uses his canoe to check in on locals remaining in the severe flooded area of Black Creek in Middleburg, Florida, on September 12, 2017. (Photo by Bastiaan Slabbers/NurPhoto/Sipa USA)(Sipa via AP Images)

Creek-side home in Middleburg, Florida, on September 13, 2017. Residents of homes near Black Creek, Clay County, return to find homes submerged by historic 28.5-foot flooding after Hurricane Irma took an unexpected turn and caused major damages in the region. (Photo by Bastiaan Slabbers/NurPhoto/Sipa USA)(Sipa via AP Images)

A major tributary of the St. Johns River, the 13-mile long creek — split into the North Prong and South Prong that merge in Middleburg — meanders through Clay County ordinarily at a tranquil pace enticing fishermen, kayakers, canoeists and other boaters as well as those simply seeking serenity by sitting on a dock watching the abundant wildlife drawn to the creek.

Irma's fury spawned flood waters that topped out at 28.5 feet on both the North and South prongs Sept. 12, easily eclipsing the previous 24.3-foot record set in 1923.

Named for its water color, which results from tannin produced by decaying vegetation and leaves, Black Creek is reddish in shallow areas, while the deeper water appears black. It's long been considered one of Florida's cleanest creeks.

The hurricane choked it with debris — partially sunken boats to jagged chunks of broken wooden docks, water-logged clothes and household trash. The flotsam-filled muddy flood waters have receded.

Both North and South prongs looked calmer this week as the water flowed past a hodgepodge of brick ranch-style homes, vacation homes on stilts and double-wide trailers lining the creek banks — often side by side, or within the same block.

The dull "thunk" of a hammer busting up soggy dry wall, and buzz of chainsaws biting into downed trees was muffled but could still be heard amid the hum of dragonflies and croaking of creek frogs.

At least 1,200 homes, county officials estimate, were in the broad swath cut by the creek's roiling flood waters.

Homes perched on high ground historically safe from flooding, at best were cut off, or at worst were submerged to their roof lines.

Some residents have flood insurance but others don't. Those without it cite the high cost, as well as assurances from prior owners, neighbors and history showing the creek had never risen high enough to flood their homes.

Among hard hit areas in Middleburg were Black Creek, Begonia and Sandy Run drives on the South Prong, and Wisteria Lane, Scenic Drive, and near Yvonne Terrace on the North Prong.

## Lives Shattered

"It's beautiful out here, when it's not all destroyed. It's really a gorgeous place but not so much right now," De St Jeor said of his two-story, farm-style home nestled in woods along the South Prong.

The creek is about 100 yards from their back porch. The couple never thought the home would flood because it had stayed dry in past storms, said De St Jeor, an information technology programmer.

"When we bought this house, pretty much everyone was saying, we guarantee you it's never going to flood ever. It's way too high up. Water has never come up anywhere near this high. They were wrong," Ana De St Jeor said.

Nonetheless, they kept the home's flood insurance although they could have asked for an exemption.

Because of her late stage pregnancy, the De St Jeors evacuated well ahead of the hurricane. Before leaving, they moved the baby's crib, playpen, clothes, car seat and other necessities down from the second to the first floor. It was a

precaution, De St Jeor said, against hurricane winds ripping off the roof and letting in the rain.

They returned home to find at least five feet of water filled the first floor. Everything for the baby was gone or ruined. The couch floated. The refrigerator was dislodged by the rushing water likely polluted with septic tank waste.

Learning of the couple's plight via social media, the women of the Clay Hill Clothes Closet at Clay Hill Church of God of Prophecy came to the rescue — throwing her a baby shower to replace all the items that were ruined, Ana De St Jeor said.

The woman and others, many who were strangers until now, have come to help them, are "nothing short of heroes" De St Jeor said.

Irma hit as the couple were two weeks away from signing a lease to open an upscale restaurant in Middleburg. They were storing restaurant and kitchen equipment in their garage and workshop. Flood waters submerged it all, as well as their second car. An artist as well as a baker, Ana De St Jeor also lost all her watercolor and acrylic paintings in the flood.

Ana De St Jeor said amid her initial shock, she questioned whether they should stay on Black Creek. Now, those doubts are gone, the couple said.

"When we first moved here, everybody told us about creek life. There had been a flood the year before and I remember the people saying they weren't going to move. Ana and I thought that was crazy, but now we get it," De St Jeor said.

## Memories Swept Away

Brightly painted, and bathed in the warming sunlight, the Noah's Ark figurines rested carefully along with a few family pictures and pieces of china on a plastic table cloth spread on the grass in the backyard of the modest house that Glenn Sr., 87, and Alta Mattox, 81, have called home for 25 years.

A high-water mark of dried mud, insect remains and crumpled leaves sits about three-quarters of the way up the outside walls, bearing silent witness to the flood waters that swamped the Black Creek Drive home.

Red Mattox said the water was about a half-foot deep inside the home and coming up fast when his parents and brother, Mark, who lives with and takes care of them, and a 71-year-old aunt with special needs, evacuated Sept. 11.

"By the time we got Momma out, she was waist deep in water trying to get her across the road," Red Mattox said.

A neighbor from across the road brought his father's boat up to the front porch of the Mattox home to ferry them to higher ground. It took three trips, and the U.S. Coast Guard to ensure their safety, he said.

"In times like this, I think people tend to pull together and do what they can for folks any how even if you don't really associate with them any other time," said Red Mattox of Clay Hill.

Married 64 years, his parents refused to evacuate earlier, arguing the creek never seeped in the home before, said Mark Mattox, who is one of four siblings in the family.

"If it was up to Momma, she would have moved in the very next day," Red Mattox said of his mother, who suffered a stroke Sept. 16, likely triggered by the storm stress. His parents are staying with family until they can move back into the four-bedroom home, he said.

Mark Mattox emphasized they are eager to return. The family sold 40 acres in Starke so his parents could buy the creek home, so his father, disabled in an industrial accident many years ago, can fish off the dock every day.

"This place means happiness for my father and my mother," Mark Mattox said. "My Dad loves to fish, and my mother loves the church she goes to here. There is no place like home."

The brothers salvaged some of their mother's Noah's Ark collection, a few family photos and a couple other items. Pretty much everything was ruined in the house, they said.

The flood also destroyed their mother's piano — a beloved gift from their father to her about 50 years ago, Red Mattox said.

"That was one of the things she was most worried about. We couldn't save it. ... So, we buried it under the [debris] pile so she couldn't see it," he said.

Sweat soaking their sky-blue T-shirts and covered in dry wall dust, volunteers from HopeForce International hauled wheelbarrows full of debris from the Mattox home Tuesday. A team of eight volunteers specializing in disaster response from the nonprofit based in Brentwood, Tenn., traveled to Black Creek to help residents.

"Mainly, what we do in these situations is we come in and take the dry wall and insulation out," said volunteer Suzanne Stroud. "It doesn't take but a few days for the mold to set in."

The Mattox brothers praised the volunteers, saying their help will make it easier to restore his parents' home. Their parents had flood insurance, but no insurance for the home's contents. It's unknown how much it will cost to replace it all, Red Mattox said.

## "Creek People Now"

Justin and Karen Hawkins moved into their dream house four months ago. The kayaking enthusiasts went from a land-locked Oakleaf apartment to a spacious three-bedroom home on Begonia Bluff perched above the South Prong.

A kayak barn, boat house and dock made the idyllic location even better for the couple expecting their first child in May.

"It was the perfect house. Four months ago," Justin Hawkins said.

Then came the nightmare of Irma. The couple rode out the horrific hurricane in their new home, along with their two dogs, and his parents who believed it was safer than theirs on Fleming Island.

"We're on a really high bluff. ... We're probably about 35 feet above the water. The creek came up almost 30 feet and it nearly reached our house," he said. "We finally started getting nervous and started putting sand bags by the back door."

Ground water got into the house from the bottom in a partial basement soaking carpet and walls. The howling wind blew off the home's chimney siding, letting in a lot of water, Hawkins said.

"We lost our boat house, our dock, our boardwalk that goes from our house all the way to the water, our kayak barn and our shed," said Hawkins, 32, who works for a defense contractor. Karen Hawkins, 30, is a fifth-grade teacher.

The storm ripped away three kayaks Hawkins had secured together with cable.

"They floated up over the trees and then went down into the woods about three houses down,"

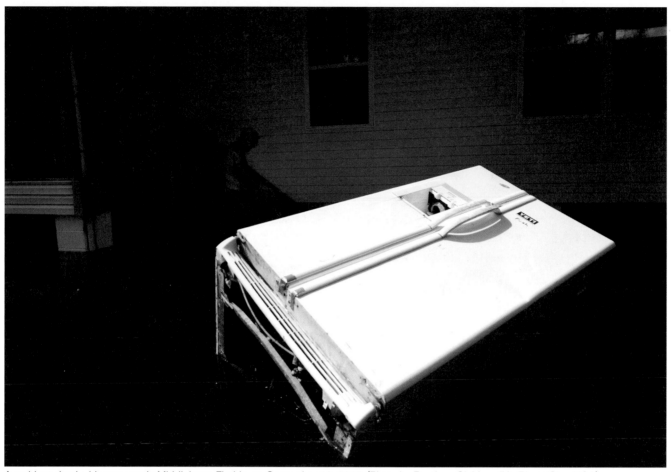

A resident checks his property in Middleburg, Florida, on September 12, 2017. (Photo by Bastiaan Slabbers/NurPhoto/Sipa USA) (Sipa via AP Images)

he said. They recovered two but one remains missing. They also found some of their paddles up in a tree, he said.

The storm also left them without electricity for several days, so they couldn't get water from their well. Nonetheless, he said they fared a lot better than most.

"We're definitely going to stay. I guess just add flood insurance now," said Hawkins, explaining they weren't required to have it because the back porch of their house was at the line of the flood zone. So, flood insurance wasn't mandatory.

"All the neighbors we've talked to, nobody has flood insurance but all were affected by the flood one way or another," he said.

Living on the creek, he said, is special.

"One of the first things we did when we moved in was just sit on our dock and just stuck our feet out over the water and took a picture of our feet. And we hung up a sign shortly after that saying 'just another day in paradise,'" Hawkins said of the peacefulness afforded by the creek.

"It's really peaceful to come home and go out back by the water and relax," he said.

Hawkins said they've met more of their neighbors following the storm than before because people keep stopping by to check on them and offering help. In turn, they have been helping their neighbors.

"Yes, I think we are creek people now. We got our wings coming through this storm," Hawkins said. ∎

© 2017 The Florida Times-Union

# IRMA RELIEF PACKAGE EXPECTED TO COST BILLIONS

## Local leaders look to Washington for aid

By Zac Anderson

*Sarasota Herald-Tribune* | Tribune News Service | September 13, 2017

Flooded homes along the Myakka River, a crumbled stretch of Manasota Beach Road, the missing roof on the Anna Maria City Pier — U.S. Rep. Vern Buchanan took it all in during an aerial tour of Hurricane Irma's damage Tuesday as he prepared to make the case for a strong federal aid package for Florida.

Buchanan's assessment after viewing the storm's aftermath in Sarasota and Manatee counties from 300 feet above in a Bell 407 helicopter: "It could've been a lot worse."

Lifting off from the Venice Municipal Airport in a Sarasota County Sheriff's Office helicopter, Buchanan circled his district to get a sense of Irma's impact. There was little obvious storm damage that was visible from the air.

What he saw was a lot of rooftops that remained intact. The exposed roof beams of the Anna Maria pier was one of the most glaring examples of Irma's power, along with homes surrounded by Myakka River floodwaters off Border Road in Venice, the

Gov. Rick Scott assesses flooding damage over Jacksonville, Fla., during the aftermath of Hurricane Irma on Sept. 12, 2017. (AP Photo/John Raoux, File)

Federal Emergency Management Agency Administrator Brock Long, center left, sitting next to Homeland Security Acting Secretary Elaine Duke, center right, speaks during a briefing at FEMA headquarters on the response to Hurricane Irma, in Washington, Sunday, Sept. 10, 2017. (AP Photo/Susan Walsh)

submerged roads at Myakka River State Park and a section of Manasota Beach Road that lost a lane to the Gulf of Mexico.

Irma inflicted relatively minor damage to buildings and infrastructure in Sarasota or Manatee counties. But Buchanan expects a massive clean-up bill and is talking to congressional leaders and White House officials about an Irma relief package.

"We're going to fight to get whatever assistance is available, every dollar," Buchanan said.

As Florida leaders turn from storm preparation to recovery, federal assistance will be critical.

The total cost of Irma is expected to be in the billions. Congress recently approved a $15.25 billion relief package to help the Houston region recover from Hurricane Harvey.

Florida Gov. Rick Scott asked the Federal Emergency Management Agency to declare all 67 counties in the state eligible for federal Irma relief money.

FEMA has agreed to help local governments in every county pay for the cost of storm preparation and recovery efforts. Another nine counties, including Sarasota and Manatee, have been approved for assistance funds that are paid directly to individuals.

Buchanan's office is encouraging Sarasota and Manatee residents who incurred disaster-related expenses to register with FEMA. The individual assistance program helps pay for a variety of disaster costs, everything from medical bills and lost medication to housing and childcare expenses.

Individuals can register at www. DisasterAssistance.gov or call 1-800-621-FEMA.

"There's really two stages," Buchanan said of the storm response. "The first is making sure people stay safe. Now we want to get them back on their feet."

Businesses impacted by the storm also may be eligible for assistance through the U.S. Small Business Administration.

Buchanan worries that the ongoing power outages are costing businesses revenue and leaving employees without paychecks.

"There are a lot of people who live paycheck to paycheck who clearly will need support, as will small businesses," he said.

Buchanan rode out Irma at the Manatee County Emergency Operations center. He's been sleeping at his brother's place in Lakewood Ranch. His home on Longboat Key lost power during the storm. He's heading back to Washington, D.C., later this week to work on a host of issues, including Irma relief.

The aerial damage assessment will help him make the case for a robust federal response, Buchanan said. As the helicopter cruised up the coast from Venice, passing over beachgoers on Siesta Key and Lido Key, Buchanan talked about the importance of securing beach renourishment funds for the eroded coastline.

At the turquoise waters off Anna Maria the pilot turned east, passing over the exposed interior of the Anna Maria pier and heading up the Manatee River before circling back over Lakewood Ranch and flooded areas along the Myakka River.

The fact that Irma did not take anyone's life in Sarasota or Manatee counties and inflicted relatively minor damage to buildings and infrastructure is great news, Buchanan said. Now the focus is on getting the community back to normal.

"This is a team effort, a community effort," he said. "And we all need to pull together." ∎

© 2017 Sarasota Herald-Tribune

Residents at La Perla community in Old San Juan comfort one another as the community recovers from Hurricane Maria, in San Juan, Puerto Rico, Monday, Sept. 25, 2017. The island territory of more than 3 million U.S. citizens is reeling in the devastating wake of Hurricane Maria. (AP Photo/Carlos Giusti)

# PART 4

# PAIN IN PUERTO RICO

"MARBELLA"
VENTA DE INTERNET & WIFI

# HURRICANE MARIA SLAMS INTO PUERTO RICO

# Category 4 storm ravages island

### By Dinah Voyles Pulver

*The News-Journal* (Daytona Beach) | Tribune News Service
September 20, 2017

Hurricane Maria made landfall over Puerto Rico Wednesday morning as a "potentially catastrophic" Category 4 hurricane.

With sustained winds of 155 mph at its core, the hurricane is traveling over the island after making landfall in the southeast coastal town of Yabucoa. Maria is expected to punish the island with life-threatening winds for 12 to 24 hours, forecasters said.

"This is going to be an extremely violent phenomenon," Gov. Ricardo Rossello said. "We have not experienced an event of this magnitude in our modern history."

At 3:14 a.m. gusts of up to 69 mph were reported in San Juan, the National Weather Service reported. By 6:30 a.m., the Weather Service reported two radars were down on the island and a gust of 113 mph (182 kph) was reported in the capital of San Juan, according to the U.S. National Hurricane Center in Miami.

The hurricane completed an eyewall replacement cycle just before making landfall, which reduced its central winds down to 155 mph, the National Hurricane Center said. The eye diameter, which had been only 10 miles across had widened to 30 miles across.

Even though continued weakening is forecast over the next few days, the Hurricane Center said Maria is expected to remain a "large and powerful hurricane" as it moves past the northern coast of the Dominican Republic and the southeastern Bahamas.

Metal roofs were already flying and windows were breaking as the storm approached before dawn, with nearly 900,000 people without power and one tree falling on an ambulance.

Streets flood as Hurricane Maria approaches the coast of Bavaro, Dominican Republic, Wednesday, Sept. 20, 2017. The U.S. National Hurricane Center says Maria has lost its major hurricane status, after raking Puerto Rico. But forecasters say some strengthening is in the forecast and Maria could again become a major hurricane by Thursday. (AP Photo/Tatiana Fernandez)

Those who sought shelter at a coliseum in San Juan were moved to the building's second and third floors, reported radio station WKAQ 580 AM.

The Hurricane Center warned that the winds around high-rises and along the windward sides of hills and mountains would be higher than the 155 mph sustained winds reported at the surface of the storm.

Forecasters are fairly certain of Maria's path over the next three days but after that, as it moves north of Florida, a few of the computer models they use to forecast predict the storm could move a little more westward, possibly taking it closer to the coastal Carolinas than originally forecast, but still well offshore.

At 8 a.m., the Hurricane Center said the center of Maria was about 15 miles south-southwest of San Juan, with 150 mph winds, making it a strong Category 4 hurricane.

Maria is forecast to move to continue moving toward the west-northwest at about 10 mph, tracking across the island before emerging off the northern coast this afternoon.

The storm had been predicted to cause a storm surge of 6 to 9 feet along the Puerto Rican coast and in the U.S. Virgin Islands, near and to the east of where the storm made landfall. That surge was expected to raise the tide as much as 4 to 6 feet above normal high tide levels in the Dominican Republic as well.

The surge is forecast to be accompanied by large and destructive waves that would raise water levels as much as 10 to 15 feet above normal tide levels in the Southeastern Bahamas and the Turks and Caicos.

As much as 25 inches of rainfall is forecast for isolated locations of Puerto Rico, with widespread rainfall of between 12 to 18 inches.

An additional 8 to 12 inches of rain also is forecast in the Virgin Islands, the eastern and northern Dominican Republic and Turks and Caicos. ■

© 2017 The News-Journal (Daytona Beach)

Rescue team members Candida Lozada, left, and Stephanie Rivera, second from left, Mary Rodriguez, second from right, and Zuly Ruiz, right, embrace as they wait to assist in the aftermath of Hurricane Maria in Humacao, Puerto Rico, Wednesday, Sept. 20, 2017. (AP Photo/Carlos Giusti)

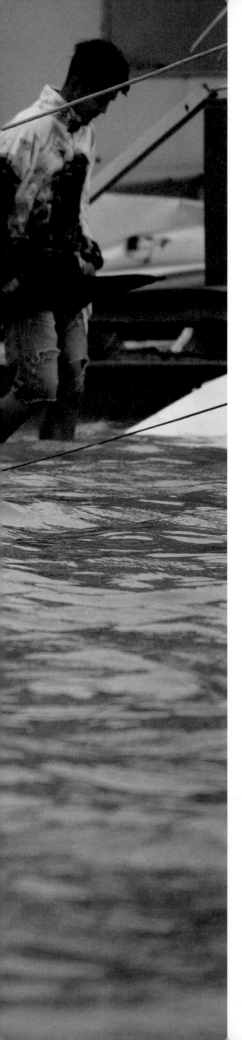

# PEOPLE WITH TIES TO PUERTO RICO: "WE WATCH, WE PRAY"

## Mainland friends and family wait for news

By Chick Jacobs

*The Fayetteville Observer* (North Carolina) | Tribune News Service
September 20, 2017

Carlos Omar Santiago was on the phone, trying to calm his mother-in-law in Puerto Rico, when the line went dead.

"That was around 7 o'clock," Santiago said from his home in Spring Lake. "We have heard nothing since."

Across the Cape Fear region, people with ties to Puerto Rico have been desperately searching for scraps of information Wednesday as major Hurricane Maria lashed the islands with sustained winds up to 145 mph. Maria's winds and torrential rain raked Puerto Rico, destroying communication towers and knocking down land lines.

"There is nothing that we have been able to learn since then," said Angie Malave. A native of Puerto Rico now living in Fayetteville, Malave worked in San Juan, the island capital, which was facing a direct hit from the storm.

"Now it's like biting nails," she added. "We watch, we pray: What else can we do now?"

People walk next to a gas station flooded and damaged by the impact of Hurricane Maria, which hit the eastern region of the island, in Humacao, Puerto Rico, Wednesday, September 20, 2017. (AP Photo/Carlos Giusti)

It had already been a storm-laden summer in Puerto Rico. Hurricane Irma gave the island a glancing blow on its way to landfall in Florida. Irma knocked out electricity on parts of the island.

"Some of my family had just gotten power back from Irma a couple of days ago," said Wanda Collazo, who grew up in the coastal town of Bayamon, near San Juan. "We also have people from the other islands who evacuated to Puerto Rico after Irma destroyed their homes.

"Now they are all there as Maria is hitting."

News comes in snippets from video, from Facebook posts by friends with family on the islands. There is a risk that some of the news may not be accurate but, Collazo says, any news is welcome.

"I have not heard from my family since 4:30 this morning," she said. "We are posting everything we can share. But no one has heard from people on the island."

That revelation, according to Malave, is even more nerve-wracking.

"While we don't know what's going on, we still know more than our families do in Puerto Rico. Just imagine being there, surrounded by all the storm and confusion, not knowing anything beyond where you are."

Collazo was able to briefly get in touch with a long-time friend on the island by cellphone. "One of my high school classmates was in the dark, asking me where the eye of the hurricane was," Collazo said. "I was her only way of getting information. So I sent her a radar image, just before we lost each other.

"We try not to worry, but how can you not?"

Malave said she continues to send texts and notes, even though she has no idea if they'll be received.

"I don't know if they're getting the notes, but I want them to know we have them in our hearts," she said. "Right now, people are frustrated. They can do nothing until the winds die down.

"The best thing we can do is pray for the safety of people there and make preparations to help as soon as we can." ∎

© 2017 The Fayetteville Observer (North Carolina)

Socorro Marques, 78, a resident at the Aires de Manantial home for low-income elderly people, holds hands with fellow resident Manuela Libran in Trujillo Alto, Puerto Rico, Wednesday, Oct. 4, 2017. (AP Photo/Carlos Giusti)

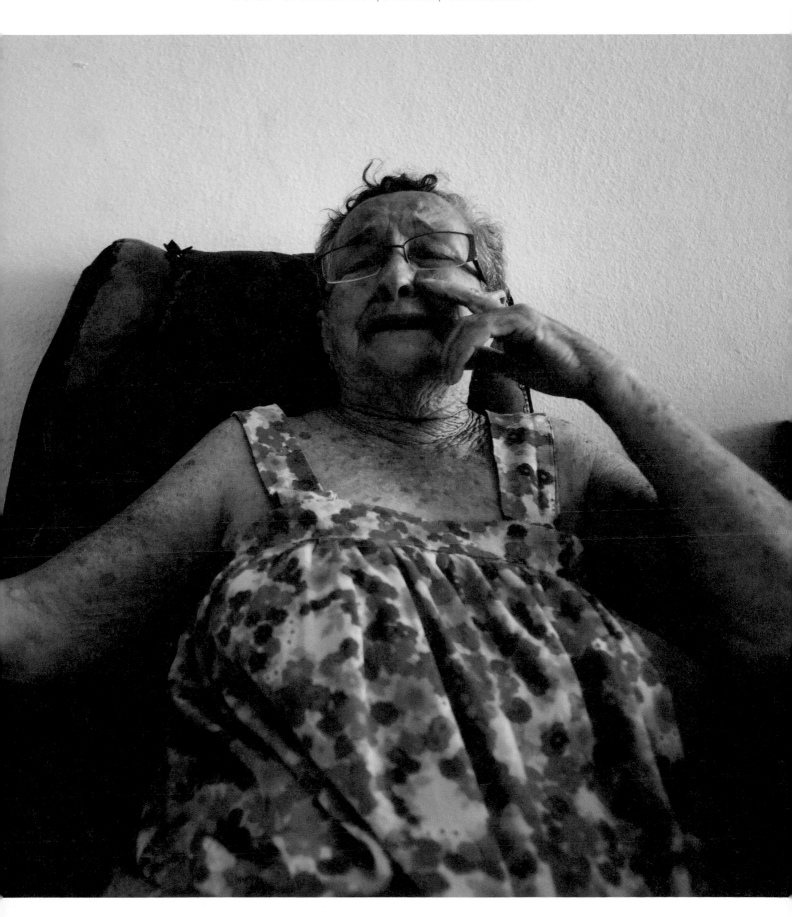

# MARIA DOWNGRADED, BUT **DAMAGE TO PUERTO RICO IS SEVERE**

## "Puerto Rico isn't going to be the same"

By Molly Hennessy-Fiske and Kurtis Lee

*Los Angeles Times* | Tribune News Service | September 20, 2017

SAN JUAN, Puerto Rico — Hurricane Maria left a historic trail of destruction across Puerto Rico on Wednesday, its powerful winds carving holes in the walls of 300-year-old homes, flooding neighborhoods, sucking metal roofs off buildings, downing 100-year-old trees and leaving the entire island without power.

In the capital of San Juan, volunteers sprang into action, assisting stranded drivers, cutting and removing downed limbs to clear the roads. Looters also took advantage of the chaos following the storm to break into furniture stores and gas stations, running past a San Juan police car with sofas and chairs. The police car did not appear to stop.

Maria made landfall as a Category 4 hurricane packing 155-mph winds — just 2 mph short of Category 5 status — near the southern city

In this Thursday, Sept. 21, 2017 photo, the home of Ashley Toledo's mother lays in ruins after the passing of Hurricane Maria in the Punta Diamante area of Ponce, Puerto Rico. A humanitarian crisis grew Saturday in Puerto Rico as towns were left without fresh water, fuel, power or phone service following Hurricane Maria's devastating passage across the island. (AP Photo/Jorge A Ramirez Portela)

of Yabucoa. But by Wednesday afternoon, the storm had been downgraded to a Category 2, according to the National Hurricane Center in Miami. It was continuing its westward march toward the Dominican Republic.

Throughout Puerto Rico — from San Juan to rural towns — roads turned into raging rivers, and social media showed people wading through chest-high water to safety. Trees that had survived innumerable storms snapped in half in the howling winds. Palm trees, stripped of their fronds, looked like matchsticks.

"Puerto Rico isn't going to be the same," said Migdalia Caratini, a lawyer who lives east of San Juan. "It's going to be before Maria and after Maria."

The island was already reeling from Hurricane Irma, which passed the northern coast of Puerto Rico last week as a Category 5. Though Puerto Rico escaped a direct hit from Irma, the storm inflected major damage on the electrical grid, and portions of the island had been without power even before Maria made landfall.

On Wednesday, officials from the Puerto Rico State Agency for Emergency and Disaster Management said that portions of the island could be without power for several weeks.

More than 500 people evacuated to the Roberto Clemente Coliseum in the capital, where pieces of the roof began to give way and leak at the height of the storm early Wednesday. As winds howled outside, Lydia Gonzalez said she watched in horror as the roof stretched and strained "like bubble gum." But it held.

A boy sits by a flooded area at the Ingenio community after the passing of Hurricane Maria, in Puerto Rico, Friday, September 22, 2017. Because of the heavy rains brought by Maria, thousands of people were evacuated from Toa Baja after the municipal government opened the gates of the Rio La Plata Dam. (AP Photo/Carlos Giusti)

# The devastation of Maria, the first Category 4 hurricane to hit Puerto Rico in 85 years, will be a further blow to the island's economy, which is anchored by the tourism industry.

"This roof was like a miracle. We heard the hurricane and thought we would see it" come apart, she said.

The winds died down briefly, and staffers moved most of the evacuees to halls on the second floor.

Gonzalez and dozens of others had to stay on cots in the dark, flooded first floor hallways because they could not handle the stairs. Gonzalez is elderly, and was caring for her 94-year-old mother, who lay on a cot, complaining of thirst. Gonzalez didn't want to give her too much water because then she would have to use the bathrooms, she said, which had not been cleaned, and the stench reached where her mother lay in the hall.

The power had gone out overnight, along with the air conditioning, and the humidity left the walls damp. Other elderly and disabled evacuees sat nearby in the darkened hall in wheelchairs. At least one lay on a stretcher.

Gonzalez, who retired from working for a local electric company, has relatives in Florida, Maryland and North Carolina, but her mother couldn't handle the plane ride and refused to leave behind their sixth-floor apartment, which they had been told to evacuate. They had stayed home during Hurricane Irma, but had to move afterward to a hotel for a week because they couldn't endure the heat without power. Gonzalez expects they and many others may be stranded for days again.

Puerto Rico Gov. Ricardo Rossello, in a statement, called for calm and "prudence during these difficult days." Citing the need to maintain public order, Rossello imposed a curfew for the island from 6 p.m. until 6 a.m. that will be in effect until Saturday.

Maria was the third major storm, after Harvey and Irma, to form in the Atlantic in recent weeks and reach Category 5 status.

On Monday night it raked the island of Dominica in the eastern Caribbean with sustained winds of 160 mph. Maria also prompted evacuations from the U.S. Virgin Islands, which already sustained significant damage from Irma. Many Virgin Island evacuees had fled to Puerto Rico.

There were no immediate reports of any deaths in Puerto Rico on Wednesday, but The Associated Press reported that Maria had killed nine people across the Caribbean. Other Caribbean islands, including St. Martin and

Barbuda, had already seen most of their housing stock destroyed by Irma.

Nearly 3,200 U.S. government staffers overseen by the Federal Emergency Management Agency were already in Puerto Rico on Wednesday helping with recovery efforts in the Caribbean after Hurricane Irma hammered the region last week. Even so, first responders were not expected to help right away — officials had said they planned to shelter indoors when winds reached 50 mph.

The White House said in a statement that President Donald Trump is continuing to monitor the situation and that he and first lady Melania Trump "send their thoughts and prayers to all those in harm's way."

Caratini, the attorney, had rented a room at the Sheraton Hotel in Old San Juan to weather the storm. Staff members barricaded doors with lumber and sandbags, activated a generator to keep electricity running on the main floor once it went out in the rest of the nine-story building, and played hurricane coverage on a big-screen television as owners walked evacuated dogs.

"The big thing is not the wind and the rain — it's the aftermath," said Caratini, whose house is near the beach.

She worried about those living in the center of the island, where many homes are made of wood and have zinc roofs that were probably ripped apart by the hurricane.

Puerto Rico has been struggling economically, and leaders had planned to reduce public workers' hours, shifting money from local to federal coffers, Caratini said. She hopes those changes get suspended, at least immediately after the storm.

For years, the commonwealth has struggled with debt. In May, Rossello said the Puerto Rican government would go to federal court in hopes of receiving protection from creditors. The U.S. territory is embroiled in a more than $70 billion debt crisis, after multiple creditors filed lawsuits trying to recuperate millions of dollars invested in government bonds.

The devastation of Maria, the first Category 4 hurricane to hit Puerto Rico in 85 years, will be a further blow to the island's economy, which is anchored by the tourism industry.

At the Sheraton, some had evacuated from other Caribbean islands where they had already survived Irma earlier this month.

"This is better than the last one," said Ken Wild, 63, an archaeologist with the National Park Service who hid in his hillside basement on the Virgin Island of St. John during Irma only to see the windows blown out. He survived along with his Doberman, Anabell, and so did his boat.

But he didn't think the boat would survive Maria, which pummeled the Virgin Islands on Tuesday night.

In San Juan on Wednesday, Rosa Avalo recalled the horror before sunrise. Avalo awoke at about 4 a.m. to find 3 to 4 inches of water had entered her 300-year-old home, Casa Lila, where she runs a business teaching tourists to make cheese.

She called to her 18-year-old son, who agreed to leave as soon as he took a shower: "That's when he started screaming."

The storm had punched a hole in their bathroom wall several feet wide, large enough that they could see winds lashing a historic fort across the street. They ran to a neighbor's house, where they planned to stay for the near future.

"I never thought it would happen to me, but now I don't have a house," she said as she stood in her doorway facing a cracked wall. "Brace yourselves because I never thought I would lose my house. I thought my house was like a bunker."

The area was without power, cellphone and internet service. She was still waiting to hear from relatives in central Puerto Rico, including her 16-year-old daughter, Anna, who was staying with her father in Manati. "I hope they're safe," she said. ■

*Hennessy-Fiske reported from San Juan and Lee from Los Angeles.*

# "TOTAL DESTRUCTION" IN PUERTO RICO

## Most of island without electricity

By Molly Hennessy-Fiske and Kurtis Lee

*Los Angeles Times* | Tribune News Service | September 22, 2017

REPORTING FROM SAN JUAN, PUERTO RICO — Gregmarys Garcia stood atop the home she shares with her two sons, ages 5 and 3, and five other relatives. The house was surrounded by thigh-high water.

The family had stockpiled bottled water and food, packing their freezer with ice. But when Hurricane Maria hit, they lost water and, like the rest of Puerto Rico, power.

Now, in their neighborhood of Las Palmeras in San Juan, whole blocks had been turned into islands. Garcia's block was inundated, including the family's three cars. They relied on a neighbor's battery-powered radio for news.

"The governor said it's total destruction in Puerto Rico, but the worst is in the west and east," she said.

And the worst wasn't over.

At least 4 to 8 inches of additional rain were expected Thursday, with up to 35 inches in isolated spots, according to Mike Brennan, a specialist at the National Hurricane Center in Miami.

"That will exacerbate the ongoing flash flooding situation that's occurring over that entire island," he said on Twitter.

Maria, the strongest storm to strike Puerto Rico in more than 80 years, reduced homes to heaps of splintered wood and crumbling concrete, turned streets into rivers of churning brown water and left the island without power.

Disaster in Yauco, Puerto Rico, after the passage of Hurricane Maria. (GDA via AP Images)

"Typically, the rain and flooding is the principal cause of deaths," Gov. Ricardo Rossello said during a Thursday briefing. "If you don't have to be out in the streets, don't."

The full extent of the damage in Puerto Rico remained unclear, as dozens of areas were still incommunicado late Thursday. Rossello said restoring power and communication networks was a top priority, and he acknowledged the frustration of islanders unable to reach family and friends — including the governor himself.

"I haven't been able to communicate with my parents," he said.

Maria had moved out of the area Thursday but remained a Category 3 storm, expected to approach the Turks and Caicos Islands and the southeastern Bahamas overnight, according to the National Hurricane Center.

For several days, Maria has pummeled the Caribbean, killing dozens, including at least 15 people in Dominica, where Prime Minister Roosevelt Skerrit said 20 more remained missing Thursday.

President Trump described Puerto Rico as "absolutely obliterated."

"Puerto Rico is in very, very tough shape," Trump said ahead of a meeting Thursday at the U.N. General Assembly, adding that he's working with Rossello on the recovery.

"It's incredible the power of that wind," Trump said. "That was very unique. Not for many decades has a storm hit a piece of land like that."

Trump signed a federal disaster declaration for the U.S. territory of 3.4 million people.

On Thursday weary and shellshocked residents began the long process of cleaning up.

In the oceanfront settlement of La Perla, several dozen people picked their way down

Lines of cars and people with gas cans form to get fuel from a gas station in the aftermath of Hurricane Maria, in Aibonito, Puerto Rico, Monday, Sept. 25, 2017. (AP Photo/Gerald Herbert)

# At the foot of Ft. San Cristobal, just outside the walls of Old San Juan, Diego Rivera chopped at a palm tree with a machete. The fort had survived since the 1700s. All around was disorder.

rocky hillsides strewn with debris to salvage what they could from the wreckage.

At the foot of Ft. San Cristobal, just outside the walls of Old San Juan, Diego Rivera chopped at a palm tree with a machete. The fort had survived since the 1700s. All around was disorder.

Rivera, who grew up here listening to elders tell stories about the explorers who discovered and christened the area La Perla, or "The Pearl," gestured to the mix of shingles, glass and lumber studded with rusty nails that littered the hillside under gray skies still threatening rain. Everything felt damp.

"We have to start cleaning this stuff, throw it away," he said, adding that the government hasn't done anything.

Rivera was clearing a path to the flooded cinder-block house where he weathered the storm. Winds tore at the metal hurricane shutters as he huddled inside, panicked. Transformers exploded outside. He tried to flee, but the downed palm tree blocked the door, leaving him trapped for about 10 hours.

The retired construction worker escaped unharmed, but his house was still full of water, the concrete ceiling crumbling. Neighboring homes of his mother, sister and niece were roofless, stripped bare by violent winds that lashed the shanties clustered above a narrow strip of beach.

Downhill, neighbors were clearing the main road. Shirtless men pushed aside stalled cars and examined ruptured water pipes as women tucked back downed power lines and swept up shattered glass.

A parking garage had collapsed on several cars. Restaurants such as Al Sabor de Sonia y Algo Mas were no longer selling mofongo and fried plantains; their doors were blocked by downed roofs. The local health center and Head Start office were covered with pieces of adjacent buildings. A sign in the park warning residents to keep the area clean had been knocked down.

Rivera said his relatives were staying in emergency hurricane shelters with hundreds of others displaced by the storm.

"All Puerto Rico is damaged," he said, but, "we lost everything here."

Rescues were ongoing, said Rep. Jenniffer Gonzalez-Colon, Puerto Rico's representative in Congress.

Flash-flood alerts sounded all day in the capital of San Juan, which saw spotty rain. Airports in San Juan, Aguadilla and Ponce were shut, and a curfew from 6 p.m. to 6 a.m. remained in effect for the island.

Near San Juan airport, drivers struggled to make their way around flooded highways and downed trees.

Across from Garcia's house, a few restaurants and an ATM machine were operating, with long lines. But most businesses were still shuttered, some of their windows broken by looters overnight.

Standing on a flooded street next to a park strewn with downed trees, Maribel Rodriguez said the curfew imposed by the governor was necessary.

"It's a good idea because yesterday it was stressful: People went right in the grocery store and took everything," said Rodriguez, 47.

She worried about relatives elsewhere in the city, whom she couldn't check on without phone or Internet service. Like Garcia, she depended on a neighbor's radio for news. Her supply of food and water was already dwindling.

Her wife, who works at Chili's restaurant, wasn't sure when it would reopen. She held a blue barrel they had just salvaged from floodwaters and hoped to use it to collect rain.

"The government just says we have to wait 72 hours" for help, she said. Of the barrel, she said, "It's stealing but ...we need it."

Across the island, people were banding together.

Pedro Rivera said one elderly woman with a heart condition needed medical attention after the storm. Neighbors called an ambulance, and when it wasn't able to reach the village because of blocked roads, they helped her up the hill so she could be taken to a hospital.

Rivera pointed to a man cracking the limbs of a downed tree to clear a side street.

"It will rise again," Rivera, 46, a cook at nearby Fresh Bistro, said of his neighborhood. "We are a village. We will raise ourselves."

Elsewhere, 8-year-old Jovanio Lopez returned with his mother Thursday after evacuating before the storm to find their home flooded. The bathroom roof was gone.

"The house broke. Everything broke," the third-grader said. "It stinks inside."

They left to stay with friends, taking what they could save, including books and his game of Monopoly.

Neighbor Sonia Viruet, 61, said the government should send crews to La Perla immediately. Beside her, a neighbor in work gloves was making slow progress gathering fallen shingles.

"We need help restoring the community. First, we need help cleaning. We can try to do it ourselves, but it will take too long," Viruet said.

Joseph Cotto took his family of six — including a 1-year-old son — to a shelter during the hurricane, but returned after the storm to help rebuild, and make space in the shelter for those in greater need.

"There are people who don't have roofs. We wanted to make room for them. We have a house," he said — although it, too, is damaged and without utilities.

Cotto, 31, a laborer for the city's public works department, figured it would take at least two months to restore power and water. On Thursday, he cleared roads and hauled seawater from the bottom of the hill to run his toilet.

Angel Marcano was also cleaning up his home Thursday. Marcano, 45, who works as an aide to autistic students, was still staying at a temporary shelter at City Hall nearby, but wasn't sure how long it would last. He also missed his La Perla neighbors, including an elderly woman across the street whom he checks on each morning.

Far down the hill near the water's edge, neighbor Ivan Lopez helped others examine damage to their homes. It was his aunt who had to be taken to the hospital, where he said she was recovering Thursday.

Lopez, 51, survived the storm in his concrete apartment, which was relatively unscathed. The handyman planned to stay to help rebuild and said he believed the government would eventually send workers to help.

"It's just the first day. They always come, bit by bit," he said.

For Lopez, like many of his neighbors, evacuating La Perla was not an option.

"Here I was born," he said, "and here I will die." ■

*Hennessy-Fiske reported from San Juan and Lee from Los Angeles.*

# More rain and flooding threatens residents

By Molly Hennessy-Fiske and Kurtis Lee

*Los Angeles Times* | Tribune News Service
September 21, 2017

REPORTING FROM SAN JUAN, PUERTO RICO — Puerto Rico, already inundated with heavy rains unleashed by Hurricane Maria, braced itself for several more inches of rain and possible flash floods while wide swaths of the island remained without power.

As the strongest hurricane to hit the island in generations continued to barrel through the Caribbean on Thursday, the full extent of the damage in Puerto Rico remained unclear, as dozens of municipalities had lost all communication. Even so, officials on the island said recovery efforts would begin promptly to help those reeling from Maria's devastation.

Mike Brennan, a specialist at the National Hurricane Center in Miami, said the storm is expected to dump at least 4 to 8 inches of additional rain and up to 35 inches in isolated spots on the island on Thursday. On Wednesday, some roads in Puerto Rico were turned into raging rivers, and people walked through chest-high brown water to safety.

National Guardsmen arrive at Barrio Obrero in Santurce to distribute water and food among those affected by the passage of Hurricane Maria, in San Juan, Puerto Rico, Sunday, Sept. 24, 2017. Federal aid is racing to stem a growing humanitarian crisis in towns left without fresh water, fuel, electricity or phone service by the hurricane. (AP Photo/ Carlos Giusti)

# A STUNNED PUERTO RICO

# BEGINS TO RECOVER

"We're still seeing heavy rainfall occurring over Puerto Rico," Brennan said in a video posted on Twitter. "That will exacerbate the ongoing flash flooding situation that's occurring over that entire island."

Flash flood alerts sounded all day in the capital of San Juan, which saw spotty rain.

Jenniffer Gonzalez-Colon, Puerto Rico's representative in the U.S. Congress, said rescue efforts are ongoing.

"Some families have been rescued, others still need help," she said on CNN on Thursday. "A lot of the communications towers are off line, so people on the mainland trying to call families and friends here on the island should know that we don't have communications in so many areas. That's the main problem right now."

Gov. Ricardo Rossello said Maria was the "most devastating storm to hit the island this century, if not in modern history."

The island's energy grid took such a severe blow from Maria that restoring power to everyone may take months, he told CNN.

The U.S. territory has been through a long recession and is deeply in debt and has a state-owned power grid that is "a little bit old, mishandled and weak," Rossello told CNN.

"It depends on the damage to the infrastructure," he said. "I'm afraid it's probably going to be severe. If it is ... we're looking at months as opposed to weeks or days." ∎

*Hennessy-Fiske reported from San Juan and Lee from Los Angeles.*

© 2017 Los Angeles Times

Jose Garcia Vicente holds a piece of plumbing he picked up, as he shows his destroyed home, in the aftermath of Hurricane Maria, in Aibonito, Puerto Rico, Monday, Sept. 25, 2017. (AP Photo/Gerald Herbert)